GEMINI

The Transfiguration of

BENNO BLIMPIE

Two Plays by
ALBERT INNAURATO

GEMINI

The Transfiguration of
BENNO
BLIMPIE

James T. White & Company
Clifton, New Jersey

GEMINI

The Transfiguration of
BENNO BLIMPIE

GEMINI

CHARACTERS

FRAN GEMINIANI is forty-five, working class, boisterous, and friendly. He is slightly overweight, coughs a lot from mild emphysema.

FRANCIS GEMINIANI, his son, is about to celebrate his twenty-first birthday. He is also plump, a little clumsy, is entering his senior year at Harvard.

LUCILLE POMPI is Fran's lady friend, very thin, early forties, working class, but strives hard to act in accordance with her ideas of ladylike behavior and elegance.

BUNNY WEINBERGER, the Geminiani's next-door neighbor, is a heavy-set blowsy woman, about forty, once very beautiful and voluptuous, now rough talking and inclined to drink too much.

HERSCHEL WEINBERGER, her son, is sixteen, very heavy, asthmatic, very bright, but eccentric. He is obsessed with Public Transportation in all its manifestations, and is shy and a little backward socially.

JUDITH HASTINGS, Francis' classmate at Harvard, is a month or two younger than Francis. She is an exceedingly, perhaps even intimidatingly, beautiful WASP. She is extremely intelligent, perhaps slightly more aggressive than she should be, but is basically well meaning.

RANDY HASTINGS, her brother, has just finished his freshman year at Harvard. Like Judith, he is a quintessential, very handsome WASP.

The play takes place on June 1 and 2, 1973. The latter marks Francis' twenty-first birthday.

ACT ONE
Scene 1: June 1, 1973. Early Morning.
Scene 2: That Evening.

ACT TWO
Scene 1: June 2, 1973. Morning.
Scene 2: That Evening.

The setting shows the backyards of two adjoining row houses in the Italian section of South Philadelphia. They are small, two-story, brick houses typical of the poorer sections of most big cities. In one house live the Geminianis, Fran and Francis, and in the other the Weinbergers, Bunny and Herschel. In the Geminiani yard is a fig tree, and along one side a high alley fence with a gate. The Weinberger yard contains an old ladder, a rusty, old tricycle, garbage cans, and a certain amount of general debris, and is also bounded by an alley wall, behind which is a high utility or telephone pole.

Gemini was first performed in a workshop production at Playwrights Horizons, and was later presented at the PAF Playhouse, Huntington, N.Y., before being produced by the Circle Repertory Company in New York City. On May 21, 1977, it opened at the Little Theatre, New York City, produced by Jerry Arrow and Jay Broad representing the Circle Repertory Company and the PAF Playhouse. It was directed by Peter Mark Schifter and had a setting by Christopher Nowak, costumes by Ernest Allen Smith, and lighting by Larry Crimmins, with the Broadway production being supervised by Marshall W. Mason. The cast in order of appearance was:

Francis Geminiani	ROBERT PICARDO
Bunny Weinberger	JESSICA JAMES
Randy Hastings	REED BIRNEY
Judith Hastings	CAROL POTTER
Herschel Weinberger	JONATHAN HADARY
Fran Geminiani	DANNY AIELLO
Lucille Pompi	ANNE DeSALVO

ACT ONE

SCENE 1

The sound of garbage men emptying the garbage in the alley. They are making an immense noise. It is just past dawn and they are banging lids, overturning cans, and yelling to one another.
Francis Geminiani appears at his bedroom window. He is dressed in a Tee shirt, his hair is wild, his glasses are awry. He has just been awakened and is in a rage.

FRANCIS: Shut up! Will you please shut up! Why aren't you men more civilized? Oh Jesus Christ!
(*He sets a speaker on the window sill, and turns on full blast the final portion of Isolde's narrative and curse from Act 1 of* Tristan und Isolde. *Bunny Weinberger appears at the second floor window of her house. She is in a torn nightgown and faded robe, and is also in a rage*)
BUNNY: Francis! Francis! Why are you playing that music at six o'clock in the mornin'? You got somethin' against my gettin' a good night's sleep?
FRANCIS: (*Leaning out his window*) Do you hear the garbage men?
BUNNY: Sure. They're just doing their job. That's the trouble wit you college kids—got no respect for the working man. Besides, I got an uncle out there.
(*Shouts out to alley behind fence*)
Hi ya Uncle Jerry!

VOICE: (*From behind the fence*) Hi ya, Bun!

BUNNY: How's your hammer hanging?

(*Then to Francis*)

See, I got connections. You stick wit me kid, I'll get you a job.

(*A knocking is heard at the front door of the Geminiani house*)

And now you got them knockin' at your door. You woke everybody up. Ain't you gonna answer it?

FRANCIS: I'm going back to bed.

(*He takes the speaker off the sill*)

BUNNY: Good. Maybe we'll have some quiet.

(*She disappears inside her bedroom. The knocking continues. The garbage men fade away. Francis has now put on a very quiet passage from Act IV of Verdi's I Vespri Siciliani. After a moment, a knocking is heard at the gate in the fence, the entrance to the Geminiani yard. Francis does not come to his window. More knocking. A pause. Then a rolled up sleeping bag comes sailing over the fence, followed by a small knapsack. Randy Hastings appears at the top of the fence. He climbs over and jumps into the yard. He looks around. Suddenly a large knapsack, the kind that has an aluminum frame, appears at the top of the fence. Randy takes it, and puts it down on the ground. Next we see a rolled up tent, a second sleeping bag on the fence, then a tennis racquet, and then Judith Hastings. She perches on top of the fence, looks around, and then jumps into the yard. Randy has piled everything neatly together in the middle of the yard. They are both in worn jeans and sneakers. They circle about the yard, peeking into Bunny's part curiously. Judith notices the fig tree and smiles. She knocks at the back door. No answer. Randy tries to open it, but it is latched from the inside. He then peeks into the window Left of the door and sees Francis sleeping in his room. He smiles at Judith, and they climb into Francis' room*)

JUDITH AND RANDY: Surprise! Surprise!

(*The music stops. Francis leaps out of bed*)

JUDITH: (*Inside the room*) Put your glasses on, it's Judith . . .

RANDY: . . . . and Randy. What's the matter?

FRANCIS: What are you doing here?

JUDITH: Come to see you, of course—

FRANCIS: Why?

JUDITH: It's your birthday tomorrow, your twenty-first.

(*At this moment, Herschel dashes out of the back door of his house and into the yard. He hurls himself onto the rusty tricycle and making subway engine noises, careens about the yard*)

RANDY: (*Looking through screen door*) Francis, who's that?

FRANCIS: (*With Judith in kitchen window*) Herschel next door.

RANDY: What's he doing?

FRANCIS: Hey Herschel, what are you doing?

HERSCHEL: I'm pretending I'm a subway engine.

FRANCIS: Which one?

HERSCHEL: Three nineteen AA four six five AA BZ substratum two. Built in 1945, in April, first run on Memorial Day.

FRANCIS: Herschel is into Public Transportation.

(*Bunny comes out of her house, still in the same torn and smudged nightgown and housecoat. She has a quart beer bottle in one hand, and a cigarette in the other*)

BUNNY: What the fuck's goin' on out here, hanh? Why you up so early?

(*Herschel, making engine noises, heads right for her. She sidesteps the tricycle easily*)

Jesus Christ, it's that engine you're goin' a see.

FRANCIS: (*From window, still with Judith. Randy has come out to get a better view*) Bunny, these are friends of mine from school. Judith Hastings and her brother, Randy.

(*Indicates Bunny*)

This is my neighbor, Bunny Weinberger.

BUNNY: I didn't know they had girls at Harvard.

FRANCIS: Judith is at Radcliffe.

BUNNY: This is my son Herschel. He's a genius. He's gotta IQ of 187 or 172, depending on which test you use.

(*To Herschel, who is still careening about*) Stop that fuckin' noise! He's also got asthma, and he tends to break out.

HERSCHEL: (*To Randy*) You want to see my collection of transfers?

RANDY: (*With a shrug*) Sure.
(*Herschel dashes into his house*)

BUNNY: (*Looking after him*) Well, all geniuses is a little crazy. You kids look hungry, so damn skinny.
(*She is poking Randy in the stomach*)

RANDY: Do you think so?

BUNNY: I guess you're scholarship students at Harvard, hanh? Although Francis is on scholarship you wouldn't know it to look at him. You wan' some breakfast?

JUDITH: That would be very nice.
(*Bunny starts for her door*)

FRANCIS: Get the roaches out of the oven first, Bunny.

BUNNY: (*Good-naturedly*) Oh, go fuck yourself. I ain't had a live roach in here in a year, unless you count Herschel, I think he's part roach. Whatayas want? Fried eggs and bacon alright?

RANDY: Sure.

BUNNY: He's normal, at least.
(*She goes inside*)

FRANCIS: So . . . you're just here for the day?

JUDITH: For the day? Some people go away to the beach from the city, we have come away to the city from the beach.

RANDY: Can you say that in French?

JUDITH: (*Coming out of the house*) Il ya des gens qui va . . .

FRANCIS: (*Interrupting*) How'd you get here?

JUDITH: We hitchhiked, of course.

FRANCIS: You rich people are all crazy. It would never occur to me to hitchhike.

JUDITH: That's because you couldn't get picked up.

RANDY: Come on, Judith, you can help me set up the tent.

FRANCIS: (*From his room, putting on his pants*) Tent?

RANDY: Sure. We always sleep outside. We could put it up under this tree. What kind is it?

JUDITH: Fig, idiot.

RANDY: What's a fig tree doing in your yard?

FRANCIS: (*Coming out of house, pants on, but barefoot*) You'll have to ask your father, he planted it. But look, I don't want . . . I mean . . . well, you see, it's my father. I mean you can't stay here. He doesn't like company.

RANDY: But I thought wops loved company.

(*Judith hits him*)

FRANCIS: Mafia.

JUDITH: The Mafia?

FRANCIS: You know, the Black Hand, Cosa Nostra, the Brother-hood . . .

RANDY: Your father's in the . . .

FRANCIS: Hit man.

JUDITH: Oh, come on!

FRANCIS: He offs Wasps. It was bred into him at an early age, this raving hatred of white Anglo-Saxon Protestants, they call them white people.

RANDY: (*Looks worried*) White people?

FRANCIS: He collects their ears after he murders them, he has a collection in his room . . .

(*Starts picking up their camping equipment and hands it to Judith and Randy*)

I'll tell you what, let's go to the bus terminal, I'll finish getting dressed, we'll put your stuff in a locker, I'll show you around, we'll take a few pictures, then you can go back later tonight. I'll get my camera.

(*He runs inside*)

RANDY: You mean we have to carry this junk around some more?

JUDITH: (*At Francis' window*) Why don't you come back with us —we've got plenty of room—mother will love you—you can cook for us.

FRANCIS: (*Appears at window*) I can't. I have a job.

RANDY: You can watch me work out.

JUDITH: Oh, Randy, grow up! I wanted to see you . . .

FRAN: (*Offstage*) Yo, Francis, you home!

FRANCIS: Oh, Jesus Christ!

(*Randy is trying to escape for his life. Judith is holding him back*)

FRAN: (*Offstage, yelling*) Yo, Francis, we're back!

(*Fran unlocks the gate, which had a chain and padlock. He appears with an empty trash can, Lucille right behind him, holding three freshly-pressed shirts on hangers. Fran sets the trash can under his kitchen window, and then notices the visitors in his yard. Yelling into window*)

You got company?

JUDITH: (*Hastily*) My name is Judith Hastings, and this is my brother Randy. We know Francis from Harvard.

FRAN: Oh yeah? I'm his dad. I didn't know Igor had friends. He just sits around all day, no job, nothin'. My name's Francis too.

(*Turns to Randy*)

But you can call me Franny, or Fran, or Frank.

(*Turns to Judith*)

And you can call me honey, or sweetness and light, or darling, whatever you like.

(*Indicates Lucille, who is trying to blend into the fence, because she has been surprised in a housecoat*)

This is Lucille.

LUCILLE: Oh, dear.

JUDITH: Well, we were just leaving.

FRAN: Leavin'? But you just got here, you can't leave.

LUCILLE: (*Attempting elegance*) Well, Fran, thanks for comin' over . . .

(*She hands Fran his shirts*)

Of course I was rather surprised, it's bein' so early, my dress.

BUNNY: (*Appears in her window*) Hi ya Fran.

FRAN: Yo Bun.

BUNNY: (*Sees Lucille*) I see you got The Holy Clam wit you. I'm cookin' breakfast.

LUCILLE: (*To Judith and Randy, still explaining*) And then I have to wash my hair . . .

BUNNY: Shut up, Lucille, you keep washin' it and it's gonna fall out, and not just your hair. Hey you kids, you wan' some oregano in these eggs?

FRAN: Why? They're still gonna be Irish eggs.

BUNNY: I gotta Jew name, but I'm Irish. Real name's Murphy.

FRAN: You still got roaches in that oven?

(*Coughs from emphysema, then laughs*)

BUNNY: You still got rats up your ass?

LUCILLE: Bunny!

(*Then to Fran*)

Stop smoking, hanh?

BUNNY: (*In her window, with a mixing bowl, singing*)
　"Oh I got plenty of nothin'
　　And nothing's got plenty of me
　　Got my butt
　　Got my boobs
　　Got my cup of tea
　Ain't no use complainin'
　　Got my butt
　　Got my boobs
　　Got my boobs!"

(*Dialogue continues over Bunny's song*)

FRAN: (*To Randy and Judith*) You just get here?

JUDITH: You're sure you want us to stay?

FRAN: Whataya mean am I sure?

RANDY: We're Wasps . . .

FRAN: So? I'm broad-minded. Is that a tent?

RANDY: We like to sleep outside.

FRAN: You kids is all nuts, you know that? So put it up!

(*Scratches*)

LUCILLE: (*Setting up a lawn chair*) Stop scratching that rash.

FRAN: That's my fig tree, you know! I planted it.

LUCILLE: (*To Bunny, who is singing "Got My Boobs"*) Bunny!
(*She sits down. Bunny is now screeching her final "Got My Boobs."
Lucille jumps up*)
Bunny!
(*Bunny laughs, and goes back to cooking. Lucille, with the situation
under control, sits down for a chat*)
So how do you do? My name is Lucille Pompi. I have a son at Yale
and my daughter is a dental technician, she works at The Graduate
Hospital, special shift, and my late husband . . .

FRAN: *Sta'zit'*, Lucille, these kids look hungry. You must be on
scholarship at Harvard, though Francis is on scholarship you'd never
know it to look at him. We got lots of food in, only thing that keeps
him from jumpin' out the window when he's home.
(*Indicating Francis' room. Coughs*)

LUCILLE: Turn away from people when you cough, hanh?
(*Randy and Judith are pitching the tent under the tree*)

FRAN: We got brebalone and pepperoni, how 'bout some while
horseshit finishes up the eggs? We also got pizzel. Francis loves them
but I got a whole box hid.

JUDITH: Oh, I'm sure breakfast will be more than enough.

FRAN: But you don't understand. That's gonna be a Irish breakfast
—that's a half a egg, a quarter slice a bacon . . .
(*Scratches*)

LUCILLE: (*Genteel*) The Irish mean well but they don't know
how to eat.
(*To Fran, genteel manner gone*) Don't scratch that rash!

FRAN: I'll get everything together.

JUDITH: I'll help you.

FRAN: Well, thank you sweetheart. What's your name again?

JUDITH: Judith.
(*He lets her go in first and admires her figure. He shakes his head
appreciatively and winks at Randy who winks back laughing. Randy
continues pitching the tent*)

LUCILLE: (*To Randy, after Fran and Judith have exited*) My son, Donny Pompi, is at Yale, he's a sophomore on the basketball team and in pre-med. He's on a Branford Scholarship. Do you know him?

RANDY: I go to Harvard.

LUCILLE: But he's at Yale. Wouldn't you know him?

RANDY: No, I go to Harvard.

LUCILLE: Is there a difference?

FRAN: (*Coming out of the kitchen, yelling*) Yo, Francis! Where's your manners? Was you raised in the jungle?
(*Fran and Judith come into the yard, he is carrying a typing table with a tray of food on it, and she has a cake and napkins*)
Sometimes I wonder about him, his mother used to say when he was born he broke the mold, maybe she was right.
(*Lucille starts serving, and repeating absentmindedly after Fran*)
Now, we got here: Coffee cake . . .

LUCILLE: Coffee cake . . .

FRAN: Jelly donuts . . .

LUCILLE: Jelly donuts . . .

FRAN: Black olives, green olives, pitted black olives—they're easier to digest, chocolate-covered donuts—
(*He holds one up*)
—they're Francis' favorites so eat them first and save him some pimples—
(*Lucille is embarrassed*)—brebalone, pepperoni, pizzel, biscuits, a fiadone Lucille baked last week and some hot peppers. Don't be shy.
(*He gives Lucille a squeeze*)

RANDY: Thanks.

FRAN: Yo, Francis! Where the hell are you?

BUNNY: (*Enters carrying a huge tray of food*) Here's breakfast.
(*She is followed out by Herschel, who is carrying a huge box. Bunny notices that the Geminiani tray is on a typing table, so she sets her tray on a trash can that is under her kitchen window, and drags the whole thing to the centre of the yard. She hands Randy a plate with a fried egg on it*)

HERSCHEL: (*To Randy*) Here's my collection of transfers.

RANDY: Lot of them.

(*Sits down in front of tent to eat*)

HERSCHEL: (*Following Randy*) Four thousand seven hundred and twenty-two. They start at eighteen seventy-three.

BUNNY: Biggest collection in the state outside of a museum. That's what my uncle works at the PTC told me.

HERSCHEL: (*Opening one of the albums*) These are from the old trolleys; they're my favorites, they're buried, you see.

FRAN: Yo, Francis!

FRANCIS: (*Inside, yelling*) Jesus Christ in Heaven, I'm coming.

FRAN: That's my Ivy League son.

FRANCIS: (*Entering the yard*) Lot of food.

FRAN: These kids gotta eat. Looka how skinny they are. You don' gotta eat, but that's all you do.

BUNNY: (*About Herschel, who is gulping large quantities of food*) This is another one. Looka him put that food away. Slow down!

(*Herschel chokes*)

Oh, oh, he's gonna have a asthma attack. I think he does it to punish me. You ever try to sleep with someone havin' a asthma attack in the next room? Drives you bananas.

(*To Herschel, still gulping*)

Take human bites for Christ' sake! Jesus, it's like a threshing machine: Varroom! Varroom!

FRAN: (*To Judith*) Don' be bashful we got plenty.

JUDITH: I'm not bashful.

FRAN: Eat then!

BUNNY: (*Lunges at Herschel with the fly swatter*) Slow down! The end of the world ain't for another twenty minutes.

(*He slows down*)

That's right.

(*She looks at his neck*)

Look at them mosquito bites. You been pickin' them? I says, you been pickin' them?

HERSCHEL: No.

BUNNY: (*Starts to beat him with the fly swatter*) I told you and I told you not to pick at them, they'll get infected.

FRAN: (*To Randy*) You got a appetite, at least.

JUDITH: (*Stands up, to Fran*) *Egli è casa dapertutto.*

FRAN: (*Not having understood*) Hanh?

FRANCIS: She's an Italian major at Radcliffe.

JUDITH: (*Very conversationally*) *Questo giardin me piace molto. Il nostro camino non furo facile, ma siamo giovane e . . .*
(*They all look at her, puzzled*)

LUCILLE: You see dear, that's Harvard Italian. We don't speak that.

FRAN: What did you say?

JUDITH: (*Very embarrassed, sits down*) Oh, nothing.

FRAN: You see, my people over there was the niggers. The farm hands, they worked the land. We're Abbruzzese; so we speak a kinda nigger Italian.

LUCILLE: Oh, Fran! He means it's a dialect.

BUNNY: (*Looking Fran over mock-critically*) Niggers, hanh? Let me look, let me look. Yeah, I thought so. Suspicious complexion.
(*She grabs his crotch. Lucille scowls*)

FRAN: (*To Bunny*) You're not eatin' as much as usual, Bun.

BUNNY: I'm eatin' light, got stage fright. Gotta go a court today.

FRAN: Yeah, why?

LUCILLE: Oh, Bunny, please, not in front of the kids!

BUNNY: That bitch, Mary O'Donnel attacked me. I was lyin' there, mindin' my own business, and she walks in, drops the groceries, screams, then throws herself on top of me.

FRAN: Where was you lyin'?

BUNNY: In bed.

FRAN: Who's bed?

BUNNY: Whataya mean: Who's bed? Don' matter who's bed. No matter where a person is, that person gotta right to be treated wit courtesy. And her fuckin' husband was no use; he just says: Oh, Mary! turns over and goes back to sleep. So's I hadda fend for myself. She threw herself on top a me, see, so I broke her fuckin' arm. Well, you woulda thought the whole world was fuckin' endin'. She sat there and screamed. I didn't know what to do. It was her house. I didn't know where nothin' was and she's a shitty housekeeper. So I shook her fuckin' husband's arm and said get the fuck up I just broke your fuckin' wife's arm. But he shook me off, you know how these men are, afta, so's I put on my slip, and I put on my dress and got the hell out of there. I'll tell you my ears was burnin'. That witch has gotta tongue like the murders in the Rue Morgue. Then, of all the face, she's got the guts to go to the cops and say I assaulted her. Well, I was real ashamed to have to admit I did go after Mary O'Donnel. She smells like old peanuts. Ever smell her, Lucille?

(*Lucille shudders and turns away*)

So's I gotta go to court and stand trial. But I ain't worried. I gotta uncle on The Force, he's a captain. Come on Herschel. Sam the Jew wan's a see his kid today.

(*She picks up her tray*)

LUCILLE: (*Not moving*) I'll help clean up.

JUDITH: (*Jumping up*) So will I.

BUNNY: Good, 'cause I gotta get ready to meet my judge. I'll show youse where everything is.

HERSCHEL: (*To Randy*) Do you want to see my collection of subway posters?

RANDY: (*After some hesitation*) Well, alright.

HERSCHEL: (*Following Randy into house, with his transfers*) I have eight hundred . . .

BUNNY: (*Holding door for Lucille*) Right this way, the palace is open.

(*Fran and Francis are left alone*)

FRAN: I didn't know your friends was comin'.

FRANCIS: I didn't either.

FRAN: They are your friends, ain't they?

FRANCIS: It isn't that simple.

FRAN: You kids is all nuts, you know that? It was that simple when I was growin' up. You hung out on the corner, see, and the guys you hung out wit was your friends, see? Never stopped to think about it.

FRANCIS: Those guys you hung out with were pretty quick to drop you when you had all the trouble with the bookies, and when mother left. You might say they deserted you.

FRAN: Yeah, yeah, you might say that.

FRANCIS: So then, they weren't friends.

FRAN: 'Course they was. People desert other people, don' make no difference if they're friends or not. I mean, if they wasn't friends to begin wit, you couldn't say they deserted me, could you?

FRANCIS: I guess not.

FRAN: Francis, this Judith, she's really somethin'. I didn't know you had the eye, you know?

FRANCIS: How was your trip to Wildwood?

FRAN: Well, Lucille had a fight wit Aunt Emma. That's why we came back. It was over water bugs. I didn't see no water bugs. But Lucille said they was everywhere. Aunt Emma thought she was accusin' her of bein' dirty. So we came back.

FRANCIS: Lucille is quite a phenomenon.

FRAN: She's good people, she means well. There ain't nothin' like a woman's company, remember that, my son, there ain't nothin' like a woman. You can think there is. I thought the horses was just as good; hell, I thought the horses was better. But I was wrong. But you gotta be careful of white women. I guess us dagos go afta them; hell, I went afta you mother, and she was white as this Judith, though not near as pretty. But you gotta be careful of them kinda women. A white woman's like a big hole, you can never be sure what's in there. So you be careful, even if she is a Italian major. What do you want for your birthday tomorrow?

(*They start clearing the yard, folding the chairs, putting trashcans back in place, typing table back in the house*)

FRANCIS: Not to be reminded of it.

FRAN: C'mon we gotta do somethin'. That's a big occasion: Twenty-one! I know what! You and your guests can have a big dinner out wit Lucille and me to celebrate.

FRANCIS: Oh, I think they'll have left by then.

FRAN: They just got here!

FRANCIS: Well, you know how these kids are nowadays, all nuts. They can't stand to be in one place more than a few hours.

FRAN: But they just pitched their tent under the fig tree, even. No, no, I think you're wrong. I think we're in for a visit. And I hope so, they seem like nice kids.

FRANCIS: Well, they're a little crazy; you know, speed, it twists the mind.

FRAN: Speed?

FRANCIS: Yeah, they're both what we call speed freaks. That's why they're so skinny.

FRAN: You mean they ain't on scholarship?

FRANCIS: They're on speed.

FRAN: Oh my God, them poor kids. They need some help. I'm gonna call Doc Pollicarpo, maybe he could help them.
(*Randy comes out of Bunny's house, carrying heavy books*)

RANDY: Herschel lent me his books on subways . . .

(*He sets them down in front of the tent*)

FRAN: You poor kid.

RANDY: (*Misunderstanding*) Well . . .

FRAN: No wonder you're so skinny.

RANDY: I'm not that skinny.

FRAN: Some other kid started you on it? Somebody tie you down and force it into your veins?

RANDY: What?

FRAN: Looka his eyes—that's a real strange color. I guess that proves it. You got holes in your arms too?

RANDY: What—why?

FRAN: Come here and sit down, you need rest, you need good food, have a black olive that's good for speed.

RANDY: (*Shocked*) Speed?

FRAN: And your sister too? That beautiful young girl on speed? It's a heart breaker. That stuff it works fast, that's why they call it speed.

(*Francis nods in agreement*)

You can see it rot the brain.

RANDY: But I'm not on . . .

(*Looks at Francis, understanding. Francis shrugs*)

FRANCIS: My father got it in his head you were on speed.

RANDY: I never touch it.

FRAN: (*Understanding*) Oh, yeah, let's make a fool of the old man.

(*Yelling*)

Yo, Lucille, get the hell out here.

(*To Randy*)

I'm sorry, young man, my son is a little twisted. His mother used to say when he came along he . . .

FRANCIS: (*Has heard this many times*) . . . when he came along he broke the mold.

FRAN: (*Yelling*) Lucille! I'm not gonna call you again.

LUCILLE: (*Coming out*) I'm here. And don't scratch that rash, makes it worse.

FRAN: (*Yelling*) Yo, Bun, good luck wit the judge!

(*To Lucille*)

Come on.

(*Heads toward the kitchen, turns back*)

Randy, if you're gonna smoke pot out here, do it quiet.

LUCILLE: Oh, I'm sure he's too nice a boy to . . .

FRAN: Lucille, get inna house!

(*Fran, with Lucille, enters house*)

RANDY: What's all this about speed? That's what I call a sixties mentality.

FRANCIS: Where's Judith?

RANDY: Still cleaning up, I guess.

(*Pulls out a box of joints*)

Want some pot?

FRANCIS: Why'd you come? You could have given me some warning.

RANDY: We're not an atomic attack.

(*He starts boxing with Francis*)

FRANCIS: You dropped in like one.

(*Randy starts doing push-ups*)

What are you doing?

RANDY: I've been working out every day and taking tiger's milk and nutriment . . .

FRANCIS: What about "wate-on"?

RANDY: Overrated.

(*Rolls over on his back*)

Hey, hold my legs.

FRANCIS: You want to play: "Sunrise at Campobello"?

RANDY: Smart ass, I want to do sit ups.

(*Francis kneels and gets a hold of Randy's feet. Randy starts doing sit ups*)

FRANCIS: (*Grunts*) One . . . Three . . . You weren't this bad last spring. Even though you did drag me to the gym once—I even had to take a shower—I stumbled around without my glasses, I couldn't see anything, my arms were out like Frankenstein's—they thought I was very strange.

(*He looks down at his arms*)

My arms are getting tired—and what is this supposed to do?

RANDY: (*Still lying on the ground*) I'm tired of being skinny.

FRANCIS: You aren't that skinny.

RANDY: I'm grotesque looking. Look at my chest.

(*Lifts shirt*)

I look like a new born duck. I want pectorals, I want biceps, I want shoulders. I want people to stop sniggering when they look at me.

FRANCIS: I don't snigger when I look at you.

RANDY: (*Seriously*) You're my friend.

(*Francis rises, uncomfortable. Randy lights up a joint*)

Is there a pool around here? I'd like to go swimming.

FRANCIS: That's a good way to get spinal meningitis. Look, Randy, don't you think I'm an unlikely choice for a jock buddy?

(*Judith comes out of the house, and joins them on the stoop*)

JUDITH: Sorry that took so long, but Lucille didn't do anything, she just stood there and insisted I had to know her son. Hey, Francis, how are you going to entertain me? Is there a museum in walking distance of Philadelphia?

RANDY: That's low priority; we're going to the boat races.

JUDITH: Randy, why don't you simply realize you're pathetic, and stop boring intelligent people?

RANDY: And why don't you treat your hemorrhoids and stop acting like somebody out of Picasso's blue period . . .

(*Bunny comes out of her house. She is wearing a very tight, white, crocheted suit, and carrying a plastic, flowered shopping bag. She is dressed for court*)

BUNNY: (*Strikes a "stunning" pose*) How do I look?

RANDY: Like you can win the case.

BUNNY: You're sweet. Give me a kiss for luck.

(*Grabs and kisses him. Then yells*)

Herschel!

(*Back to Randy*)

Look at his skin, look at his eyes; ain't anybody around here looks like you, honey. Like a fuckin' white sheik!

(*Herschel enters from his house. He is dressed for a visit with his father, in an enormous, ill-fitting brown suit. He is munching on something*)

Oh, Herschel. Come on.

(*Brushes his suit roughly*)

And look you, don' you go havin' no asthma attacks wit your father, he blames me.

JUDITH: (*Suddenly*) Herschel, Randy'll go with you; he wants to go to the park and study your subway books.

(*She grabs one of the big books, and drops it in Randy's hands. Randy looks shocked*)

HERSCHEL: (*Astounded and delighted*) Really?

JUDITH: (*Before Randy can speak*) And do you happen to have, by any chance, a map of the subway system? Randy was just saying how much he wanted to study one.

HERSCHEL: Yes!

(*Digs in his pockets*)

I have three. This one is the most up to date. You're interested—really interested?

RANDY: Well—I . . .

HERSCHEL: (*Grabbing his arm*) Come on, I'll walk you to the park!

(*Drags Randy off down the alley*)

I know the way and everything . . .

BUNNY: (*Yelling after them*) Don't fall down, Herschel, that suit costs a fortune to clean.

(*To Judith and Francis*)

Well, I'm off. Wish me luck.

JUDITH AND FRANCIS: (*Smoking a joint*) Good luck.

BUNNY: (*Crosses to the gate*) I'll see youse later. I mean I hope I see youse later.

(*She exits, crossing her fingers for luck. Judith passes the joint to Francis. She goes as if to kiss him, but instead, blows smoke in his mouth. He chokes*)

FRANCIS: Did you come here to humiliate me?

JUDITH: What?

FRANCIS: What do you call coming here with your brother, climbing over the back fence, walking in on me, half-naked, unannounced? And then, Bunny, Herschel—the house is a mess—

JUDITH: That doesn't bother me, really. You oughtn't to be ashamed.

FRANCIS: Oh, I wish you hadn't come, that's all, I wish you hadn't come, you or Randy . . .

JUDITH: But why? I took you seriously, I took—everything seriously and then I hadn't heard—

FRANCIS: I didn't want any more of either of you.

JUDITH: Francis!

FRANCIS: Have you looked at me? I'm fat!

JUDITH: You're not fat!

FRANCIS: Then what do you call this?
(*Makes two rolls of fat with his hands*)
If I try I can make three—

JUDITH: You're crazy! What does that have to do with anything?

FRANCIS: No attractive person has ever been interested in me . . .

JUDITH: Well, maybe they thought you were a bore.

FRANCIS: "Love enters through the eyes," that's Dante . . .

JUDITH: And he liked little girls.

FRANCIS: Look, I don't know what you see when you look at me. I've made myself a monster—and tomorrow I'm to be twenty-one and all I can feel is myself sinking.

JUDITH: But Francis . . .

FRANCIS: Look, I don't want to discuss it now, not here, not with my father around the corner. Now I'm going into my room and play some music. Then I'm going for a walk. I would appreciate it if you'd strike your tent and gather up your things and your brother and leave before I return.

(*He goes into his room, and puts on some quiet music. Judith is left alone. Suddenly, Randy appears over the fence*)

RANDY: This is very mysterious.

BLACKOUT

SCENE 2

Scene the same. Later that day. It is early evening. During the scene night falls.

Fran is cooking spaghetti in his kitchen. He is singing "Strangers in the Night."

Randy is inside the tent.

Francis enters through the gate. Sees the tent. He slams the gate.

FRANCIS: They're still here.
FRAN: (*From inside house*) Yo, Francis, is that you?
FRANCIS: Yes.
FRAN: I'm in the kitchen.
(*Francis goes inside*)
Where have you been?
FRANCIS: Where is she now?
FRAN: In your room. Why don't you go in to see her?
FRANCIS: Didn't it ever occur to you that I don' want you to interfere . . .
FRAN: (*Smiles*) "Strangers in the night . . ."
(*Francis goes into his room. Herschel comes bounding in from the alley*)
HERSCHEL: (*To Fran*) Hi. Where's Randy?
FRAN: In his tent.
(*Yells*)
Yo, Randy! You got company. (*Randy peeks out of the tent. Herschel sits down by the tent*)
HERSCHEL: Hi. I just got back from my father's. He wanted me to stay over but I faked a petit mal and he let me go.

RANDY: A petit mal?

HERSCHEL: You know, a fit. A little one. I stumbled around and I slobbered and I told him everything was black. He got worried. I told him I left my medicine back here, so he gave me money for a cab. I took the bus.

(*Francis and Judith appear in window*)

Like, I was wondering, would you like to come with me to, like, see the engine? It's not far from here. It's alright if you don't want to come, like, I mean, I understand, you know? Everybody can't be interested in Public Transportation, it's not that interesting, you know? So, like, I understand if you aren't interested but would you like to come?

RANDY: (*Who has gotten a towel and toilet case out of his knapsack*) Can we have dinner first?

HERSCHEL: You mean you'll come? How about that! I'll go and change—I'll be right back.

(*He starts to run, trips over his own feet, falls, picks himself up, and runs into his house*)

JUDITH: (*From window*) I see you're about to be broadened.

RANDY: What could I do?

(*To Fran in kitchen*)

Mr. Geminiani!

FRAN: (*Appears in kitchen window*) Fran, it's Fran!

RANDY: Fran. Can I take a shower?

FRAN: Be my guest. You got a towel?

RANDY: Yes.

(*He goes into the house*)

FRAN: (*Comes out, yelling*) Yo, Francis!

FRANCIS: (*He and Judith are right behind him*) Jesus Christ, I'm right here.

FRAN: That's my Ivy League son. Look, once in a while when your lips get tired, go in and stir the spaghettis, hanh? I'm going to get Lucille.

FRANCIS: She lives around the corner, why can't she come over herself?

FRAN: Don' get smart and show some respect. She believes in the boogie man.

(*He throws the kitchen towel in through the window, like he was making a jump shot*)

Yes! Two points!

(*Holds up two fingers like cuckold's horns*)

"Strangers in the night . . ."

(*He exits through the gate*)

JUDITH: Lucille and your father are—well, you know, aren't they?

FRANCIS: I don't know, they drink an awful lot of coffee.

JUDITH: Stimulates the gonads—

(*She embraces Francis and kisses him. He looks uncomfortable*)

What's the matter?

FRANCIS: I'm sorry.

JUDITH: Sorry about what?

(*He looks away*)

You know, I think you are an eternal adolescent, a German Adolescent, a German Romantic Adolescent. You were born out of context, you'd have been much happier in the forties of the last century when it was eternally twilight.

FRANCIS: Do I detect a veiled reference to *Zwielicht* by Eichendorf?

JUDITH: I took Basic European Literature also, and did better than you did.

FRANCIS: You did not.

JUDITH: I got the highest mark on the objective test: 98! What did you get?

(*She laughs*)

FRANCIS: (*Bantering with her*) My SAT verbal and achievement tests were higher than yours.

JUDITH: How do you know?

FRANCIS: I looked them up in the office. I pretended to go faint, and while the registrar ran for water, I looked at your file.

JUDITH: (*Entering into his game*) I find that hard to believe; I had the highest score in the verbal at St. Paul's and also in the English Achievement Test.

FRANCIS: That's what it said alongside your IQ.

JUDITH: (*Taken aback in spite of herself*) My IQ?

FRANCIS: Very interesting that IQ. It was recorded in bright red ink. There was also a parenthesis, in which someone had written: "Poor girl, but she has great determination."

JUDITH: I find jokes about IQ's in poor taste.

FRANCIS: Then you are an adolescent, a German Adolescent, a German Romantic Adolescent.

JUDITH: And before this edifying discussion you were about to say: "Fuck you, Judith."

FRANCIS: Don't put it that way . . .

JUDITH: But more or less it was get lost, see you later, oh yes, have a nice summer—and maybe, just maybe, I'll tell you why later. You seem to want to skip that part, the why.
(*She picks up the end of a garden hose, and points it at Francis like a machine gun, and with a Humphrey Bogart voice, says:*)
Look, I came to see you, that's ballsy, now you've got to reciprocate and tell me why . . .
(*She puts down the hose, and the accent*)
Do I bore you? Do you think I'm ugly? Do I have bad breath?

FRANCIS: Oh, come on!

JUDITH: Hey, Francis, we're just alike, can't you see that?

FRANCIS: (*Indicates the house and yard*) Oh yeah.

JUDITH: Two over achievers. Really. I know my family is better off than yours; but we're just alike, and there was something last winter and now you're telling me . . .

FRANCIS: Look, I'm going to be twenty-one tomorrow. Well . . . I don't know what to say.

JUDITH: Is there a reason?

FRANCIS: I don't think I can say.

JUDITH: That doesn't make any sense.

FRANCIS: I think I'm queer.

JUDITH: Why don't we back up a bit. I said: "We're just alike et cetera," and you said you were going to be twenty-one tomorrow, and I looked at you with deep-set, sea-blue eyes, and you said . . .

FRANCIS: I think I'm queer.

JUDITH: (*Laughs*) Well, I guess we can't get around it. Do you want to amplify? I mean this seems like quite a leap from what I remember of those long, sweet, ecstatic nights, naked in each other's young arms, clinging to . . .

FRANCIS: We fucked. Big deal. That's what kids are supposed to do. And be serious.

JUDITH: I am serious. Is there a particular boy?

FRANCIS: Yes.

JUDITH: An adolescent, a German Adolescent . . .

FRANCIS: Not German, no.

JUDITH: Do I know him?

(*Francis doesn't answer*)

Reciprocal?

FRANCIS: It was just this spring. He began to haunt me. We became friends. We talked a lot—late in my room when you were studying. Well, I don't know, and you see—I've had, well, crushes before. I dreamed of him. It's not reciprocal, no, he doesn't know, but it became more and more obvious to me. I mean, I'd look at him, and then some other boy would catch my eye and I'd think—you see?

JUDITH: Well. I suppose I could start teaching you the secrets of make-up.

(*Francis turns away, annoyed*)

Well, how do you expect me to react? You seem to think I ought to leap out the window because of it. But it's like you're suddenly turning to me and saying you are from Mars. Well, you might be, but I don't see much evidence and I can't see what difference it makes. I'm talking about you and me, I and thou and all that. All right, maybe you do have an eye for the boys, well so do I, but you . . . you are special to me. I wouldn't throw you over just because a hockey player looked good, why do you have to give me up?

FRANCIS: I don't think that makes any sense, Judith. I mean, if I were from Mars, it would make a difference, I'd have seven legs and talk a different language and that's how I feel now.

(*Judith embraces him*)

Don't touch me so much, Judith, and don't look at me . . .

JUDITH: Then you're afraid. That explains that fat and ugly nonsense and this sudden homosexual panic. You're afraid that anyone who responds to you will make demands you can't meet. You're afraid you'll fail . . .

FRANCIS: Good Evening Ladies and Gentlemen, Texaco Presents: "Banality on Parade!"

JUDITH: You're afraid to venture. That's why you've enshrined someone who doesn't respond to you, probably doesn't even know you're interested. If the relationship never happens, you are never put to the test and can't fail. The Over Achiever's Great Nightmare!

FRANCIS: That's crazy!

JUDITH: I bet this boy who draws you is some Harvard sprite, a dew-touched freshman . . .

FRANCIS: He was a freshman.

JUDITH: In Randy's class and that proves it. Look at Randy—what kind of response could someone like that have but the giggles? And you know that. You're afraid of commitment. And remember what Dante says about those who refuse to make commitments. They're not even in Hell, but are condemned to run about the outskirts for eternity.

(*Francis, who has heard enough, has stuck his head inside Bunny's kitchen window, and brought it down over his neck like a guillotine. Judith now runs over to the fence, and starts climbing to the top*)

Ed io che reguardai vidi una insegna che girando correva tanta ratta,
che d'ogni posa me parea indegna . . . !
(*She leaps off the fence. Francis runs to her aid*)

FRANCIS: Judith! Jesus Christ!

JUDITH: (*As he helps her up*) You see? I ventured, I made the great leap and remained unscathed.
(*Herschel runs out of his house, dressed in his old pants and torn sweat shirt, carrying one sneaker*)

HERSCHEL: I heard a noise. Is Randy alright?

FRANCIS: Judith, you're alright?

JUDITH: Good as nude!
(*Limps over to stoop and sits*)

FRANCIS: Oh shit! I forgot to stir the spaghetti. Now they'll all stick together . . .
(*Runs into the kitchen, runs out again*)
You're sure you're alright?

JUDITH: Stir the spaghetti. We don't want them sticking together.
(*Francis goes into the kitchen*)

HERSCHEL: You're the one who fell?

JUDITH: You might put it that way.

HERSCHEL: (*Sits down beside Judith. Puts on his other sneaker*) I do that. One time I fell while I was having an asthma attack. My mother called the ambulance. She has, like, an uncle who's a driver. They rushed me to the hospital. Like, you know, the siren screaming? That was two years ago, right before I went to high school. It was St. Agnes Hospital over Track 37 on the A, the AA, the AA 1 through 7 and the B express lines, maybe you passed it? I didn't get, like, hurt falling, you know. Still, my mother asked me what I wanted most in the whole world, you know? I told her and she let me ride the subway for twelve whole hours. Like, she rode them with me. She had to stay home from work for two days.

JUDITH: (*Crosses to tent, and gets a bandana out of her knapsack. She sits down, and starts cleaning her knee, which she'd hurt in leaping off the fence*) Why are you so interested in the subways?

HERSCHEL: (*Joins her on the ground*) Oh, not just the subways. I love buses too, you know? And my favorites are, well, you won't laugh? The trolleys. They are very beautiful. There's a trolley graveyard about two blocks from here. I was thinking, like maybe Randy would like to see that, you know? I could go see the engine any time. The trolley graveyard is well, like, I guess, beautiful, you know? Really. They're just there, like old creatures everyone's forgotten, some of them rusted out, and some of them on their sides, and one, the old thirty-two, is like standing straight up as though sayin', like, I'm going to stand here and be myself, no matter what. I talk to them. Oh, I shouldn't have said that. Don't tell my mother, please? It's, you know, like people who go to castles and look for, for, well, like, knights in shining armor, you know? That past was beautiful and somehow, like, pure. The same is true of the trolleys. I follow the old thirty-two route all the time. It leads right to the graveyard where the thirty-two is buried, you know? It's like, well, fate. The tracks are half-covered with filth and pitch, new pitch like the city pours on. It oozes in the summer and people walk on it, but you can see the tracks and you see, like, it's true, like, old things last, good things last, like, you know? The trolleys are all filthy and half-covered and rusted out and laughed at, and even though they're not much use to anybody and kind of ugly like, by most standards, they're, like, they're, well, I guess, beautiful, you know?

(*Randy enters having finished his shower. He flicks his towel at Herschel*)

RANDY: Hey, that shower is a trip. I should have taken my surf board.

HERSCHEL: Like, you should have used our shower, it's in much better shape, you know? Next time you want to take a shower, let me know.

JUDITH: Well, there's one cosmic issue settled.

RANDY: (*Crosses to kitchen window*) Mmmmm. That sauce smells good.

FRANCIS: (*Appears in kitchen window*) We call it gravy.

RANDY: When will it be ready?

FRANCIS: Soon. (*Disappears inside house*)

HERSCHEL: (*To Randy*) Then we can go to the graveyard.

(*Randy looks surprised*)

See, like, I decided it might be, well, more fun, if we saw all the dead trolleys, you know, and leave the engine for later.

RANDY: Whatever you say.

(*Back to the window*)

Francis, look—is there something wrong?

FRAN: (*Offstage, yelling*) Yo, Francis! We're here.

(*Comes in from gate*)

Hi kids.

(*Going into house*)

You stir that stuff?

FRANCIS: (*From inside*) Yeah.

(*Randy gets a shirt out of his knapsack and crawls into the tent. Herschel starts crawling into the tent*)

RANDY: Herschel . . . careful!

HERSCHEL: (*Inside the tent*) I'm careful.

LUCILLE: (*Offstage*) Judith!

RANDY: Well, sit over there.

(*Herschel plops down, blocking the entire entrance with his back. Lucille comes into the yard with a sweater and jacket. She approaches Judith*)

LUCILLE: Judy, I brought you a sweater. I thought you might be chilly later tonight and I didn't know if you brought one with you.

JUDITH: Thank you.

LUCILLE: (*Puts sweater around Judith's shoulders*) It's real sheep's wool. My friend, Diane, gave it to me. Her daughter, Joann, is a model for KYZ-TV in Center City—special shift. She's a Cancer, so am I, that's why Fran says I'm a disease. My son, Donny, he's at Yale in pre-med, Branford Scholarship, I think he'll make a wonderful doctor, don't Yale make wonderful doctors?

JUDITH: I'm sure I don't know.

(*Fran comes out with Francis. He is carrying a large fold-up metal table*)

FRAN: Make yourself useful, Lucille. I got the table, go get the plates.

RANDY: (*Getting away from Herschel who is hovering around him*)
I'll help set up.
(*Lucille goes into the house, and returns with a tray, with plates, napkins, cutlery, glasses, bug spray, and a "plastic lace" table cloth*)

FRAN: How was your shower?

RANDY: I expected to see seals and Eskimos any minute.

FRAN: At least you got out of the bathroom alive. There are beach chairs in the cellar, why don't you get them? Francis, show this young man where the beach chairs is in the cellar.
(*Fran goes back into the house, Francis, Randy, and Herschel go past the house to the cellar, and Lucille starts setting the table*)

LUCILLE: You know Judy, my daughter, she's a dental technician at The Graduate Hospital—special shift. She wanted to go to Yale, but she couldn't get in. She thought it was her teeth. They're buck. She said the woman looked at her funny the whole time at the interview. Now I told her she should just carry herself with poise and forget her teeth. Y'know what she said to me: how can I forget my teeth; they're in my mouth! Not a very poised thing to say. That's why she didn't get into Yale: No poise. That's why she ain't got no husband, either. Do the people at Yale think teeth are important?

JUDITH: I don't know anything about Yale.

LUCILLE: But what do you think?

JUDITH: Yes, I think teeth are very important for success in life.
(*She is setting out cutlery*)
At the prep school I attended they had us practice our bite three times a day.

LUCILLE: (*Politely, taken in*) Oh?

JUDITH: We would bite off a poised bite, and chew with poise, and then sing a C major scale whilst we swilled the food in our mouths. I could even sing songs whilst swilling food with poise. In fact, I once sang the first aria of the Queen of the Night while

swilling half a hamburger and a bucket of french fries. . . . Of
course, remaining utterly poised, or "pwased," as we say at Harvard.

LUCILLE: Oh.

(*She walks around the table spraying insect repellent*)

It kills them very quickly.

(*Francis, Randy, and Herschel enter the yard with beach chairs and
old kitchen chairs, which they proceed to set up*)

RANDY: (*To Francis, continuing a conversation*) C'mon, Francis,
what's going on?

FRAN: (*From the kitchen*) Yo, Lucille, give me a hand!

JUDITH: I'll be glad to help.

(*Runs into the kitchen*)

RANDY: Come on, Francis, I mean I'm three years younger than
you—so tell me . . .

(*Simultaneously, Lucille and Herschel approach Randy*)

HERSCHEL: Would you like to see my models of the trolley fleet
of 1926?

LUCILLE: (*Giving Randy a jacket*) I brought you one of my son's
jackets, because I thought you might get cold later and I didn't
know if you brought one wit you. My son's girl friend bought it for
him at Wanamaker's.

(*Fran and Judith come back out*)

BUNNY: (*Calling from inside her house*) Yo! Where is everybody?

FRAN: Yo, Bun! We're out here.

(*Bunny comes stumbling out of her house. She has been drinking.
She never stops moving, constantly dancing and leaping about, she
cries out in war hoops and screams of victory*)

BUNNY: I won! I won! I wanna kiss from everybody but Lucille!

(*She goes around kissing everyone, except Lucille. She gets to
Randy*)

Oh, you're such a honey bun, I could eat you.

(*She kisses him, then grabs his crotch*)

I'll skip Francis too.

RANDY: Wanna smoke, Herschel?

HERSCHEL: Sure.

(*They sit down by the tent, Herschel sitting as far away from Bunny as possible*)

BUNNY: Break out the horsepiss, Fran!

(*Fran goes into the kitchen for liquor*)

Jesus Christ in Heaven, I won!

FRAN: (*Returns with bottle of Scotch*) How do you want it?

BUNNY: Straight up the dark and narrow path, honey.

(*She takes a swig from the bottle*)

You shoulda seen me in that courtroom, I told them all about it, that bitch didn't even have the decency to fart before throwin' herself on top of me. I coulda been ruptured for life, I says, and she's a Catholic, I couldn't believe it. Catholics got self-control.

LUCILLE: (*To Judith*) Well, good Catholics have self-control. Sister Mary Emaryd, my friend, she used to work at Wanamaker's before she married Christ. She . . .

BUNNY: (*To Randy*) That judge looked at me, let me tell you.

LUCILLE: She would allow herself to go the bathroom only twice a day.

BUNNY: (*To Fran*) I felt twenty again.

LUCILLE: (*To Judith*) She said: Urgency is all in the mind.

BUNNY: (*To Randy*) I felt like a fuckin' young filly in heat. Look, honey, you ever see my boobies swayin'?

(*She sways them for Randy. He giggles*)

LUCILLE: (*To Francis*) I go to the bathroom more than that, yet I go to Mass every Sunday . . .

BUNNY: (*To Randy*) You smokin' that killer weed, hon?

RANDY: Sure. You want some?

BUNNY: Don' need that shit. Don' need nothin' to get high, I'm high naturally. I was born floatin'.

(*She leans on table, almost knocking everything over*)

Come and dance with me, baby. (*She grabs a very reluctant Randy*) C'mon! "Flat foot floozie with the floy, floy . . ."

(They start doing the jitterbug, and Randy bumps into Bunny, knocking the breath out of her)

Fuck you world! Fuck you Mary O'Donnel! Fuck you Sam the Jew! Fuck you Catholic Church! Fuck you Mom! I won! You shoulda seen them look at me, I felt like a fuckin' starlit. My boobies swayin', and when I walked to the stand I did my strut; my fuckin' bitch-in-heat strut. Come on, Lucille, can you strut like this?

(She comes up behind Lucille, and "bumps" her. Lucille starts swearing in Italian. Bunny turns to Judith)

Come on, honey, what's your name, can you strut like this? I can fuckin' strut up a storm. My hips have made many a wave in their time, honey, many a wave! I sent out hurricanes, I sent out earthquakes, I sent out tidal waves from my fuckin' hips. Yo, Fran!

FRAN: Yo, Bun!

BUNNY: Remember when I was in that fuckin' community theatre down at Gruen Recreation Center?

FRAN: Seventeenth Street.

LUCILLE: Sixteenth and Wolf!

BUNNY: I played Sadie Thompson in that play. I let my hair grow down long. It was real long then, not dyed shit yellow like it is now. I fuckin' got hair like hepatitis now. I played that part! I hadda sheer slip on and my legs, Jesus Christ, my legs! I fuckin' felt the earth tremble when I walked, I played that bitch like Mount Vesuvius and the clappin', honey, the clappin'!

FRAN: You were a big hit, yep.

BUNNY: At the curtain call, I held my boobs out like this:

(She sticks out her chest)

. . . and they screamed, honey, those fuckin' grown men screamed!

(To Randy)

Feel 'em, honey, feel these grapes of mine. *(She puts Randy's hand on her boobs)*

RANDY: Mrs. Weinberger!

BUNNY: They're still nice, hanh? I fuckin' won that case!

(She has to sit down)

Then I married Sam the Jew and bore Herschel. Look at the fruit of my loins, look, this is one of the earthquakes I sent out of my hips. Boom! Boom! When he walks you can hear him around the corner, but he's a fuckin' genius at least. He's got an IQ of 187 or 172, dependin' on which test you use, despite his father!

LUCILLE: (*This has been building up*) Che disgraziat'!
(*She runs into the house followed by Fran*)

BUNNY: (*Looking after Fran*) I coulda had . . . well, almost anybody, more or less. I coulda been a chorus girl, then I met Sam the Kike and that was that. He had the evil eye, that Hebe, them little pointy eyes. He'd screw them up like he was lookin' for blackheads, then, suddenly, they'd go real soft and get big. I was a sucker for them fuckin' eyes. He's a jeweller, called me his jewel. Sam the Jew. I smell like old peanuts!

RANDY: (*Offering her the joint*) Sure you don't want some?

BUNNY: No, honey, I got me some coke for a giddy sniff. I get it from my uncle on the force; he gives me a discount, he's a captain.
(*She suddenly sees Herschel smoking behind the tent*)
Hey, wait a minute! You been smokin' that shit? Herschel! Have you been smokin' that shit?

HERSCHEL: (*Butts the joint quickly*) No . . .

BUNNY: Don' you lie to me. Didn't I tell you never to smoke that shit? It'll fuckin' rot your brain and you'll be more of a vegetable than you already are. God damn you, I'll beat the shit outta you!
(*She lunges for him*)

HERSCHEL: (*Scurrying out of her way*) Come on!

BUNNY: Come on???? Come on??? I'll come on, you fuckin' four-eyed fat-assed creep, I'll come on!
(*She grabs the bottle of Scotch, and chases Herschel into the house. We see them in their kitchen window. She is beating the shit out of Herschel*)
Twelve fuckin' hours! Twelve fuckin' hours I was in labor wit you, screamin' on that table and for what? To fuckin' find you smokin' dope?
(*His asthma attack is starting*)

That's right! Go ahead! Have a fuckin' asthma attack, cough your fuckin' head off! See if I care!

(*She disappears inside the house. Herschel is at the window, gasping for air, until he realizes that she has gone. His asthma attack miraculously stops. He disappears. During Herschel's attack everyone on stage stares at him, horrified. Randy passes Judith the joint. She refuses it. Francis takes a toke, and passes it back to Randy. Bunny, inside her house, is heard singing at the out of tune piano. Offstage*)

"Moon river wider than a mile
  I'm screwing up in style some day . . ."

(*Fran and Lucille come in from the house. He has a big bowl of spaghetti, and she is carrying a very elaborate antipasto*)

FRAN: (*Sitting down at the head of the table*) Well, I hope everybody's gotta appetite, 'cause there's enough to feed the Chinee army and ain't no room to keep it either.

LUCILLE: (*Sniffing the air*) I think the Delassandro's down the alley are burning their children's clothing again. That smell!

(*Randy and Francis break up, and put out the joint*)

FRAN: You all got plates, I'll serve. Francis you get the gravy pot, I'll pass the macs, we also got antipast'; made special by Lucille Pompi . . .

(*Lucille simpers*)

and Lucille Pompi's antipast' is a delicacy.

(*He gives Lucille a hug. Francis arrives with the gravy pot. Fran is serving*)

And here we got the gravy meat: Veal, sausage, lamb, meat balls, and brasiole.

(*He passes plate to Judith*)

JUDITH: Oh, that's too much!

FRAN: Your stomach's bigger than your eyes. We also got wine. Francis!

(*Randy snaps his fingers at Francis, as if to say: Hop to it. Francis goes into house for wine. Fran passes plate to Lucille*)

Lucille?

LUCILLE: No thank you, Fran, I'll just pick.

(*He passes the plate to Randy*)

Randy?

(*Lucille is busy making sure everyone is taken care of. Francis has returned and is going around the table pouring wine. Fran serves a plate to Francis*)

Francis?

FRANCIS: I'm not so hungry tonight.

FRAN: (*Keeping the plate for himself*) Oh, we better get down on our knees, we've just witnessed a miracle.

LUCILLE: Oh, Fran, don't blaspheme.

FRAN: (*Everyone is eating but Lucille*) Sure you don' wan' none, Lucille?

LUCILLE: I'll just pick out of your plate.

(*She then proceeds to pick a large piece of lettuce from Fran's plate and stuffs it in her mouth*)

FRAN: (*To Randy and Judith*) You kids enjoying your stay?

(*Lucille now gets a forkful of spaghetti from Fran's plate and proceeds to eat that*) This is your first time in South Philly, I bet. You ought to get Francis to take you around tomorrow and see the sights. Them sights'll make you nearsighted, that's how pretty South Philly is.

(*Lucille has speared more lettuce from Fran, and he grabs her wrist*)

Yo, Lucille, I'll get you a plate.

LUCILLE: (*She frees her hand, stuffs the lettuce in her mouth, and says:*) No, thank you, Fran, I'm not hungry.

(*She notices something on Judith's plate, picks it, and eats it. Judith and Randy are amazed*)

FRAN: Lucille! Let that kid alone and fill your own plate.

LUCILLE: (*With a full mouth*) Fran, I'm not hungry!

(*She sees a tomato wedge on Randy's plate. She picks up her fork, and pounces on the tomato*)

FRAN: Lucille!

LUCILLE: He wasn't going to eat that.

FRAN: How do you know?

LUCILLE: Look how skinny he is.

(*Herschel appears in his doorway*)

FRAN: Hi ya, Herschel.

(*Everyone greets him*)

You feel better?

HERSCHEL: I guess.

FRAN: Well, get a plate and sit down!

HERSCHEL: You don't mind?

FRAN: You're the guest of honor.

(*Herschel comes down to the table, to the empty chair, and starts pulling it around the table, making Francis get out of the way, until he is next to Randy. Randy, Judith, and Lucille, who are all sitting on the long side of the table have to scoot over to make room for Herschel. He sits down next to Randy*)

HERSCHEL: (*To Randy*) Can we still . . .

RANDY: Yeah, yeah, sure.

(*Fran has piled spaghetti and sauce for Herschel. He is trying to pass the plate down to Herschel, but Lucille snatches it, gets a forkful of pasta, and then passes the plate on. Everyone, except Francis, is eating*)

FRAN: Gonna be night soon. And tomorrow's my son's birthday. Seems like yesterday he was my little buddy, on the chubby side, but cute all the same, and tomorrow he's gonna be—what? Six? Gonna be a man tomorrow. Looka him squirm. Everybody hits twenty-one sooner or later, 'cept me, I'm still nineteen. Salute!

(*They all lift their glasses in a toast and drink, except Herschel, who keeps shoveling it down*)

Judith, look, you can see that fig tree wave in the wind if you squint. Francis, remember the day I planted it? I got the sledge hammer out of the cellar, people that was here before us left it, and I broke that concrete. His mother, she'd had enough of both of us, and took off headin' down south. She was like a bird had too much of winter. Met a nice Southern man.

LUCILLE: Protestant.

FRAN: They're married. Can't have kids though; she had a hyster-ectomy just before she left. It's a shame. She's good people and so's this man, she shoulda had kids wit him. He's real normal, nice lookin', don' cough like I do, don' get rashes neither, and to him, horses is for ridin'!

(*He breaks himself up. Then starts to cough. Lucille is picking out of Judith's plate. Big forkful of spaghetti*)

They'd have had nice kids. The kind that woulda made her happy. She's one of them people that like to fade inna the air. Don' wanna stand out. Francis and me, well, we stand out. Don't wanna, under-stand, but we talk too loud, cough, scratch ourselves, get rashes, are kinda big. You have to notice us. Don' have to like us but you gotta see us.

(*Lucille pats Fran's cheek lovingly*)

Well, his mother, she was good people and meant well, but she wasn't too easy wit us, she wanted a home in the suburbs, all the Sears and Roebuck catalogs lined up against the wall, and two white kids, just like her, white like the fog, kids you hadda squint to see. Well, this one day, she packed her bags, see, rented a big truck and took everything, even my portable TV.

(*He laughs at the "joke"*)

I guess it'll be cool tonight. She left me, you see, she left me. So I come out here and smash that concrete. Next day I planted the fig tree. I went to the one guy in the neighborhood would give me the time of day, borrowed thirty dollars and bought this tree, the dirt, some fertilizer . . .

(*Lucille's hand is in his plate again*)

Jesus Christ in Heaven! Lucille! Would you fill your own plate and stop actin' like the poor relative??!

LUCILLE: (*She quickly stuffs food in her mouth*) Stop pickin' on me! I ain't actin' like the poor relative!

FRAN: Whataya call pickin' at his plate, then pickin' at my plate, then pickin' at his plate, then pickin' at her plate, for Christ' sake, hanh? Stop pickin'! Take! Take wit both hands, it's there, why you act like there ain't plenty when there is, hanh? What's the matter you???!!!!

(*He has taken two enormous handfuls of spaghetti out of the bowl and dropped them into Lucille's plate*)

LUCILLE: (*Screaming*) Eh! Sta'zit'!

FRAN: (*Shaking her plate under her nose*) Mangi taci' o—

LUCILLE: (*Stands up and screams at him*) Fongoul!

(*She runs out of the yard*)

FRAN: Jesus Christ! See you kids later.

(*Yells*)

Lucille, I was only kidding!

(*Runs off after her*)

HERSCHEL: (*Rising, to Randy*) I'm finished.

RANDY: (*With a sigh*) Alright.

(*To Judith and Francis*)

See you later.

(*Herschel and Randy exit through the alley*)

JUDITH: (*Rises, starts stacking*) I'll put the dishes in the sink.

(*She suddenly drops the plates on the table*)

It's Randy, isn't it?

BUNNY: (*Stumbles out of her house. She is in her robe and night-gown again*) Hi, you two. You got some more horsepiss? I'm out.

FRANCIS: I'll look, Bunny.

(*Runs into his kitchen*)

BUNNY: You look sort of peaked, hon, upset over somethin'? A man, maybe?

JUDITH: Maybe.

BUNNY: Well, take my advice and heat up the coke bottle; men ain't worth shit, not shit.

FRANCIS: (*Coming out with a bottle*) Here, Bunny.

BUNNY: (*Takes a slug of whiskey*) You're a saint, just a fuckin' saint.

(*She collapses in a heap, completely out. Francis gets her under each arm, and Judith holds the door open. Francis starts dragging*) *her back in. Bunny, coming to for a moment:*) Shit! Why am I such a whale? Why ain't a porpoise or a dolphin? Why do I gotta be a whale wit hepatitis hair?

FRANCIS: Come on, Bunny, I'll help you inside . . .

BUNNY: You're a saint, a fuckin' saint.

(*They disappear inside Bunny's house. Francis returns immediately*)

JUDITH: You and Randy . . . !

FRANCIS: Me and Randy nothing. He doesn't know a thing about it. He's been following me around all day asking why I won't look at him. What can I say? We were friends, and he can't understand . . .

(*Randy and Herschel have re-entered from the alley*)

Well, who can understand . . .

JUDITH: What about the trolleys?

HERSCHEL: A different guard was there. We can go tomorrow though, my friend'll be there.

RANDY: (*To Judith*) What's the matter?

JUDITH: (*To Francis, indicating Randy*) Just look at him.

(*Peals of laughter*)

And look at you.

HERSCHEL: (*To Randy*) It's early yet, would you like to see my books on ornamental tiles . . .

RANDY: Good night, Herschel.

HERSCHEL: I guess everybody can't be interested in . . .

RANDY: (*Pushes him inside, and closes the door behind him*)

Good night, Herschel!

HERSCHEL: Good night, Randy.

(*Disappears inside his house*)

RANDY: (*To Francis and Judith*) Now, what's going on?

(*Judith continues laughing*)

Francis?

FRANCIS: Alright, Judith, why don't you just tell him?

JUDITH: And you don't want him told? What future is there for you if he doesn't even know? Happiness begins with knowledge, doesn't it?

FRANCIS: If it does, you are in a lot of trouble!
(*Runs into his house, slamming the door*)

RANDY: Hey look, this is unfair. What's going on?

JUDITH: I have discovered this fine day that I have a rival for the affections of one, Francis Geminiani.

RANDY: Oh yeah? I'm not surprised.

JUDITH: What?

RANDY: Well, Judy, you're kind of a bitch, you know. I mean, talking in Italian to his father and Lucille—nothing personal, I mean . . .

JUDITH: Well, you are a creep, aren't you?

RANDY: And I mean like forcing me to look at those subway books with Herschel, just so you could be alone with Francis. So who's this rival? Somebody from the neighborhood who can make good gravy?
(*He is laughing, and crawling inside the tent*)

JUDITH: (*Starts rubbing her hands together gleefully*) Well, the person in question is in the yard right now, under the fig tree, and it isn't me.

RANDY: (*Pops his head out*) What?

BLACKOUT

ACT TWO

SCENE 1

Scene the same. The next morning, about nine o'clock.

As the lights come up, Francis is seen in his window, staring at the tent. Judith is asleep in a sleeping-bag outside the tent, and Randy is inside.

Bunny comes out of her house, dressed in her ragged housecoat, she is disoriented and mumbles to herself. Francis sees her but says nothing.

She is carrying a brown paper bag. She disappears into the alley, and is next seen climbing up the telephone pole behind the alley wall. She has to stop every few rungs and almost falls off once or twice. Finally she gets to the top of the alley wall, still clutching the bag, shakes her fist at the heavens and makes to jump.

A dog is heard barking in the distance.

FRANCIS: (*Yelling from his window*) Hey, Bunny! What are you doing?
BUNNY: (*Peering in his direction, trying to bring him into focus*) Hanh?
FRANCIS: What are you doing?
BUNNY: Who's 'at?

FRANCIS: Francis next door. Come down, you'll hurt yourself.

BUNNY: What are ya, blind? You go to Harvard and can't tell I'm gonna jump?

FRANCIS: Bunny!

BUNNY: Shut up, Francis, I'm gonna splatter my fuckin' body on the concrete down there and don' wan' no interference. I thought it all out. My uncle's an undertaker, he'll do it cheap.

(*Herschel sticks his head out the second story window of Bunny's house*)

HERSCHEL: Mom! What are you doing?

BUNNY: Herschel, don' look, it'll give you asthma.

HERSCHEL: Don't jump, Mom!

BUNNY: Herschel, I gotta favor to ask of you. If I don' die in jumpin', I want you to finish me off wit this.

(*Waves the bag*)

It's rat poison. Was Uncle Eddie's Christmas present.

HERSCHEL: Mom, please!

BUNNY: You didn't scratch them new mosquito bites, did you?

HERSCHEL: No. And I took my medicine and I used my atomizer and brushed my teeth, please don't jump.

BUNNY: Good, you keep it up. Don' wan' to be a mess at my funeral.

HERSCHEL: Funeral!

(*Pulls his head in, and runs out into the yard. Judith is awake and getting dressed. Randy comes out of the tent, a little confused by the noise. Francis has come out, and is trying to coax her down*)

RANDY: What's going on?

HERSCHEL: (*Arrives, puffing, in the yard. His pajamas are disgracefully dirty, as is his robe which is much too small for him*) Please, Mom, I'm sorry, I didn't mean to do it . . .

BUNNY: What?

HERSCHEL: I don't know, it must be something I did. I'll never have asthma again, I'll stop having seizures, I'll take gym class. Don't jump!

BUNNY: (*Starts climbing higher, till she is about the height of the second story window*) Herschel, is that any way to act, hanh? Was you raised in the jungle? Show some dignity, you want the neighbors to talk?

HERSCHEL: I'll burn my transfer collection, I'll give up the subways . . .

BUNNY: Nah, that's alright, Herschel. You'll be better off in a home.

HERSCHEL: A home??!!!

(*He can hardly get the word out. He starts having an asthma attack*)

BUNNY: Jesus Christ in Heaven, he's havin' an attack! Can't I even commit suicide in peace?

JUDITH: Should I call the police?

FRANCIS: Call Lucille. DE 6-1567.

JUDITH: DE 6-1567.

(*She runs into Francis' house*)

RANDY: What about Herschel?

BUNNY: Get his fuckin' atomizer—it's in the third room on the second floor.

(*Randy runs into Bunny's house*)

Jesus Christ in Heaven! And it's all for attention.

FRANCIS: What is, Bunny?

BUNNY: His fuckin' attacks! I read them books! It's all for attention, that all these kids want nowadays. I didn't get no attention when I was a kid and look at me? Am I weird? Nah! I didn't get no asthma, I didn't even get pimples.

JUDITH: (*Appears in the kitchen window*) I get a busy signal.

FRANCIS: Busy? This time of day?

BUNNY: They think because they can fart and blink at the same time they got the world conquered.

FRANCIS: Did you get the number right?

BUNNY: That's all they want: attention!

JUDITH: DE 6-1567.

FRANCIS: Jesus! That's our number. It's DE 6-1656.

(*Judith disappears inside the house. Randy appears in the second story window of Bunny's house*)

RANDY: I can't find the atomizer!

HERSCHEL: (*Gasping, on the ground at the foot of the wall*) By the bed, under all the Kleenex!

(*Randy continues looking for it*)

FRANCIS: Come on, Bunny, climb down!

BUNNY: (*Climbing down to the top of the wall*) Education! That's these kids problems! Look at him—a fuckin' genius; and he looks like some live turd some fuckin' giant laid. Huff some more, Herschel . . .

RANDY: (*Running out of house*) I got it! I got it.

(*Herschel grabs the atomizer. His attack subsides*)

BUNNY: They all oughta be put to work! That's what happened to me. Yeah! My mom put me to work when I was ten, singin' songs for pennies in the Franciscan monastery on Wolf Street!

(*Judith comes back into the yard*)

I hadda sing for everybody—them bums, them old ladies. Once some crazy old lady made me sing "Mein Yiddische Mama" six times —then gave me a five-dollar bill. Well, even though it's a Catholic place I figured, shit, make the money. So I learned "Bei Mir Bist du Shoen" for the next week and sang it—and they beat the shit outta me. If that wasn't a birth trauma, what was! I read them books, know all about it. I've hadda shit-filled life; feel like some turd stuck in the pipe so Herschel get your fat ass outta the way, you too, hon, or I'll crush youse!

FRAN: (*Offstage, yelling*) What's goin' on out here?

BUNNY: Yo, Fran!

FRAN: Yo, Bun!

BUNNY: I'm gonna jump!

LUCILLE: (*Running into the yard from gate, in hair curlers*) Che disgraziat'! Who's gonna clean it up, hanh?

FRAN: (*Follows Lucille in*) Whataya mean you're gonna jump?

BUNNY: Whataya mean, whataya mean? I'm gonna leap off this fuckin' wall and if that don' finish me, I'm takin' this rat poison and Herschel better move or I'm takin' him with me. Jesus Christ, can't even die without his havin' a attack.

(*Fran and Francis half carry, half drag Herschel away from the wall, and lay him down on the stoop. He is screaming and kicking*)

You mean I gotta listen to that in Heaven?

LUCILLE: You ain't going to Heaven!

FRAN: Come on, be good and get down. You don't got no reason to jump!

BUNNY: I got reason, I got reason!

FRAN: Yeah, what?

BUNNY: Got nobody in the whole fuckin' world, I turned ugly, I got no money, I ain't got no prospects . . .

FRAN: That's been true of my whole life and you don' see me jumpin' off alley walls and takin' rat poison. Besides, it's Francis' twenty-first birthday today.

BUNNY: You mean there's gonna be a party?

FRAN: A big one!

BUNNY: Why didn't you say so, hanh? Get that friggin' ladder, I'm comin' down!

(*Francis and Randy run to get the ladder that has been leaning against the fence. They set it up under the wall, and help Bunny climb down. Bunny, to Randy*)

You're so strong, hon, give me a kiss!

(*Kisses him. Then she turns on Herschel, who is still wheezing and crying*)

You! Get in that fuckin' house! Makin' a spectacle of yourself wit them pajamas!

(*She chases Herschel into their house. Much shaking of heads from the others. Everyone is very tense. Francis takes the ladder back to the fence*)

HERSCHEL: (*As he is running inside*) What the fuck do you want me to do?

BUNNY: (*In her house continuing a diatribe against Herschel*) And what's this I hear from your no good father? You had a fuckin' petit mal yesterday?!

HERSCHEL: (*In the house*) No, I didn't!

BUNNY: Liar! Didn't I tell you to behave wit him?
(*Sounds of her beating him*)
I told you to act normal.

HERSCHEL: Who could act normal with you for a mother?
(*A sound like a piano falling over is heard from Bunny's house. A silence. Then suddenly, long surprised screams of pain from Herschel. Fran tries to hug Francis. Francis gets away. Bunny comes running out of her house to the stoop*)

BUNNY: You guys wanna get a piano offa Herschel?

FRAN: What's the piano doin' on Herschel?

BUNNY: He gave me some lip and I threw it on him.

FRAN: Oh, alright.
(*Kisses Francis*)
Happy birthday my son.
(*Fran and Francis run into Bunny's house*)

BUNNY: Do you think I ruptured him for life?
(*Bunny and Randy run into the house. Judith makes to follow, but Lucille stops her*)

LUCILLE: Ain't ladylike to go in there.

JUDITH: Herschel might be hurt.

LUCILLE: If that kid ain't dead yet, he's indestructible.
(*Noises from inside the house, of the piano being lifted*)
He's always fallin' down stairs, gettin' hit by cars, gettin' beat up, havin' fits, gettin' asthma, throwin' up, comin' down with pneumonia. A piano ain't gonna hurt him.
(*She sets a garden chair next to the tent*)
Besides, that piano's out of tune, how much damage could it do?

JUDITH: This is crazy! All that noise and Bunny on the wall . . .

LUCILLE: (*Sits in chair*) Happens alla the time. That's why no neighbors stuck their heads out. We're used to it around here. Tessie across the street come back from the shore last Sunday and found this burglar in her cellar.

(*Judith has gone in the tent to finish dressing*)

Judy, she ties him to an old sofa, then, wit her sister, she shoves it down the front steps. Then she sets it on fire. We come back from church and there is this sofa on the front steps wit a screamin' man on it and flames everywhere. We call the fire engine. They hose the poor bastard down and rush him to the hospital. So this mornin' was mild, believe me.

(*Judith is now sitting by the tent, putting on her sneakers*)

Do you wanna come wit me to Wanamaker's and buy Francis a present? I have a employee's discount so you can buy him somethin' real nice for less. Or did you get somethin' already?

JUDITH: Not really—a few joke things. I don't think he's gonna think they're funny.

(*She gets a brush and mirror out of her knapsack. Music is heard from Bunny's house. Bunny appears in her window, brushing her hair*)

BUNNY: Yo, Lucille! We got the piano up. You wanna come in and sing?

LUCILLE: No, Bunny.

BUNNY: Well, I'm cookin' breakfast. You wan' some?

LUCILLE AND JUDITH: No thanks.

JUDITH: How is Herschel?

BUNNY: A little purple about the shins, but he'll survive. You sure you don' wan' some breakfast?

JUDITH: No thank you!

BUNNY: You should take some lessons from your brother.

(*She disappears inside her house*)

LUCILLE: What did she mean about your brother?

JUDITH: Everybody loves Randy—EVERYBODY it seems!

LUCILLE: Well, he's nice lookin', that's for sure. But I'm not crazy about him. I never warm up to white people much. You're an exception. You got poise. You have lovely teeth.

(From inside the house we hear:)

    "I want a girl
    Just like the girl
    That married dear old dad
    She was a pearl
    And the only girl
    That daddy ever had . . . "

(Dialogue continues over this)

JUDITH: They got Francis to play the piano, all those wrong notes.

LUCILLE: Why are you interested in Francis when you're so beautiful?

JUDITH: If I hear that once more, I'm going to stick my face in acid!

LUCILLE: But why? *Perchè?* What do you see in him?

JUDITH: Why are you interested in his father?

LUCILLE: I ain't got much choice. I'm not pretty. I'm a widow. Nobody wants a widow. It's like bein' an old sheet. I might be clean and kept nice but people can't help noticin' it's been used.

(Bunny is heard singing:)

    "When Irish eyes are smilin'."

(Lucille continues over song) So I put up wit Fran. He's good people, he means well. But you know, he coughs alla the time, eats too much, makes noises, you know he's got the colitis, and them rashes! Between coughin', scratchin' and runnin' to the bathroom, I'm surprised he's got so much weight on him. Oh, well, that's my life.

(Judith offers her the brush. She is about to use it, then discreetly pulls Judith's hair out of the bristles)

But, Francis? Like father like son, remember.

JUDITH: Oh, I don't know. We talked yesterday and I was up most of the night, thinking: why? All the possible bad reasons started cramming themselves into my head. Perhaps I have sensed it all along and I was attracted to Francis because he was . . .

(Stops herself)

Well, just because he's the way he is.

(From inside the house we hear:)

　　"For it was Mary, Mary

　　　Plain as any name can be

　　　For in society, propriety

　　　Will say, Marie."

(Lucille speaks over this)

LUCILLE: You mean queer? Don't be shocked, I know what queer is.

(She turns her chair toward Judith)

I had a long talk wit my son, Donny, about it before he went off. He's at Yale, pre-med, Branford Scholarship. I warned him to be careful. My friend, Diane's husband, he's a foot doctor, they met in a singles bar, then got married because he had corns real bad, well, he told me, Yale puts out a lot of queers along wit the doctors and the lawyers. But Donny's got a girl friend, and though I think she's a pig, I guess it proves he's got some interest in the girls. But Francis? Well, Fran and me had a long talk. He's afraid for Francis. Well, I think Francis is. There ain't been no girls around here except to sell cookies. That's why Fran was so happy to see you, and wanted you to stay, even though you wanted to go. It's hard on a man to have a queer for a son. I mean, I guess Fran would rather he was queer than humpbacked or dead, still it's hard.

JUDITH: Well, I thought that might be why I was interested. He'd be safe then. But I don't think so. He and I are really alike, you see. Neither of us makes contact with people. We both goof a lot, but most of the time, that's all there is.

BUNNY: *(From inside her house)* Alright, I'm slingin' this shit on the table!

JUDITH: And there are other reasons. Just where I am, you know? I'm a romantic, I guess, and I assume there is something worth doing, that active is better than passive. But I feel on the edge of falling, or freezing.

LUCILLE: *(Shakes her head)* When I was your age—*ma-done . . . !*

JUDITH: Maybe it's harder for us, now. The war's over, no one much is ethnic anymore, there aren't many jobs. When there were marches and strikes and moratoriums, people didn't think much about the future, they were distracted, sort of a hippie bread and circuses idea.

LUCILLE: (*Nods her head, but she doesn't understand one word*) Yeah.

JUDITH: No one had time to worry about how they'd live five years from now—it was all now. Everybody could be a hero, occupy a dean's office, publish his memoirs, have them serialized in *The New York Times*—

LUCILLE: Wit the small print!

JUDITH: And you have to wonder, all that energy, and that courage, was it just adolescence? Sometimes I'm afraid. Just afraid. Maybe we're at the end of the spiral which people once thought endless. Maybe it's running out. I don't want it to be over. Francis is afraid too. But together . . . I'm sorry, I'm not making any sense, I didn't sleep much.

LUCILLE: But you didn't buy him a birthday present.

JUDITH: Is that important?

LUCILLE: Vital. It's the gesture. Don' matter what it is but you got to make the gesture. It shows respect. It shows you're serious. No birthday present and he's gotta right to wonder if you mean it. It's like an outward sign. You just can't go around sayin': I need you, or I love you and then, ignorin' them on special occasions. That don' make no sense. So you buy them the birthday present, you send them the card, you go visit them inna hospital, you bake them the cake— you show them respect. *Cabisce?* Respect!

JUDITH: *Si.*

LUCILLE: *Bene.* All you can do is try and hope. That's how I got my husband, may God forgive him, and may he rest in peace. You really like Francis? Come on, you come wit me to Wanamaker's we buy Francis a present we cheer ourselves up. (*Fran comes out of Bunny's house*)

FRAN: Yo, Lucille!

LUCILLE: Judith and me's goin' ta Wanamaker's to buy Francis a present.

FRAN: See youse later, be good and be careful.

(*Lucille and Judith exit through the gate. Francis comes racing out of Bunny's house*)

Yo, where you goin'?

FRANCIS: Nowhere.

FRAN: You got company.

FRANCIS: I didn't invite them.

FRAN: (*Embraces Francis*) Happy birthday, son.

FRANCIS: Don't hang on me so much.

FRAN: What are you afraid of? You got somewhere to go you take some coin.

(*Offers him some money*)

FRANCIS: I don't need any money.

FRAN: Well, take some more.

FRANCIS: I don't need any more.

FRAN: Take!

FRANCIS: I don't need it!!

FRAN: Look my son, I'm gonna give you a piece of advice I learned from the army, from dealin' wit your mother and from twenty years in the Printers' Union: Take! Take wit both hands, both feet and your mouth too. If your ass is flexible enough take wit that, use your knees and your elbows, train your balls and take! *Prend'—cabisce?* Somebody offers you somethin', you take it, then run . . .

(*Puts the money in Francis' shirt pocket*)

. . . but always say thank you first. And look, if there's ever anything, well, that conventional people, not like us Geminiani Italians —but other people might be ashamed of, don't ever be afraid to come to me, no matter how hard it is, I'll understand—understand?

FRANCIS: I don't understand.

(*Suddenly embraces his father*)

But I understand, okay?

(*Runs out through the gate*)

FRAN: Where you goin'?

FRANCIS: To buy some diet soda.

FRAN: That diet crap is gonna kill ya.

(*Randy comes out of Bunny's house, trailed by Herschel*)

RANDY: Where's Francis?

FRAN: He went to buy diet crap.

HERSCHEL: (*Grabs Randy's arm, and starts pulling him toward the alley*) Maybe we'll pass him, you know, like on our way to the trolleys . . .

RANDY: (*Freeing himself*) Is there a pool around here? I'd like to go swimming.

FRAN: Yeah.

HERSCHEL: You promised!

FRAN: There's a Community Center about four blocks from here, Herschel can go with you. You can change here.

RANDY: Great.

(*Randy crawls into the tent to change. Bunny comes out of her house, eating a sandwich*)

BUNNY: Hey, Herschel, I thought you was draggin' Beau Brummel to the trolleys—

HERSCHEL: He wants to go swimming.

BUNNY: Why don't you go wit him?

HERSCHEL: (*Under his breath*) Fuck!

BUNNY: Where's the birthday boy?

FRAN: He took off.

BUNNY: Helluva way to treat company. Prob'ly went to buy a opera record.

RANDY: (*Still inside the tent*) He already has thousands.

FRAN: (*To Bunny*) Look, I got stuff to do, gotta buy Francis a birthday cake. Bun, you wanna come?

BUNNY: Sure, I could use a donut or two.

(*They exit through the gate. Herschel picks up his tricycle*)

HERSCHEL: Randy, Randy!

RANDY: (*From inside the tent*) What?

HERSCHEL: Would you like to play trolley?

RANDY: How?

HERSCHEL: Just call ding, when I ask you to. Like . . .
(*Pipes out*) Ding!

RANDY: Okay.

HERSCHEL: (*Careening around the yard like a trolley, making a lot of noise*) Ritner! . . . Now.

RANDY: Ding!

HERSCHEL: Good.
(*Careens*)
Tasker! . . . Now.

RANDY: Ding!

HERSCHEL: Dickinson! . . . Now.
(*Silence*)
Now. Oh, you missed that one.
(*Randy comes of the tent, in a T-shirt and shorts*)

RANDY: Ding!
(*Herschel is gaping at him*)
Do you think I look weird?
(*Herschel shakes his head "No"*) I mean, skinny.

HERSCHEL: I think you look, like, you know—

RANDY: Yeah, yeah. But do you think my legs are too thin?

HERSCHEL: Oh, no!

RANDY: Boy, it's rough being this thin, you know, I've tried to put on at least ten pounds. I bought two quarts of this stuff called "Wate-On."

HERSCHEL: (*Points to his stomach*) Oh yeah, like "weight on"—

RANDY: Putrid stuff. I drank a quart of it, tastes like milk of magnesia, I got sick for a week and lost ten pounds.

HERSCHEL: I tried to kill myself by drinking a quart of milk of magnesia once; but I didn't lose any weight.

(*Francis enters through the gate, drinking a diet soda. A tense moment between Francis and Randy*)

RANDY: We're going swimming.

FRANCIS: I'll stay here.

RANDY: Okay, Herschel, let's go . . .

(*They start off, suddenly Randy staggers, clutches the air, twists about, acts dizzy, and falls to the ground. He is faking a petit mal*)

HERSCHEL: (*Very alarmed*) Randy, what is it?

FRANCIS: (*Catching on*) Looks like a petit mal, Herschel.

HERSCHEL: No, no, that's epilepsy. Take your belt off!

FRANCIS: Why?

HERSCHEL: So he won't bite his tongue off. Give it to me!

(*Sticks belt in Randy's mouth*) I'll go get my medicine!

(*Rushes into his house*)

RANDY: (*Who has been writhing on the ground until now, suddenly sits up*)

Are you a faggot?

(*Herschel comes running out with a bottle of medicine. Randy starts writhing again*)

HERSCHEL: Here—you have to shake it first!

FRANCIS: (*Shaking the bottle*) I think he'll need some valium too—

HERSCHEL: Good idea!

(*Runs into house, and reappears almost instantly*)

Fives or tens?

FRANCIS: Fives should do it.

(*Herschel races into house*)

RANDY: (*Sits up, dropping the fit*) I mean homosexual—I mean, gay person—

HERSCHEL: (*Racing back out*) We're out!

(*Randy fakes the fit again*)

FRANCIS: Do you have any aspirin?

RANDY: (*Mumbling unintelligibly*) Aspirin upsets my stomach!

FRANCIS: Aspirin upsets his stomach.

HERSCHEL: Tylenol?

FRANCIS: Tylenol?

RANDY: Tylenol!

HERSCHEL AND FRANCIS: Tylenol!

HERSCHEL: I'll go get some!

(*Races off through the alley*)

RANDY: (*He stands, dusts himself off, awkward pause*) When we talked and all that, you know in your room, were you just trying to make me?

FRANCIS: I don't know.

RANDY: I don't care that much, but it's worse being treated like you were laying a trap for me. And I didn't think you were gay—odd maybe. Have there . . .

(*He realizes how silly this is going to sound*)

. . . been many before me?

FRANCIS: Well, starting in high school there was Max. He was a poet, a Libra, on the fencing team, short and dark, compact you might say, very dashing with his èpèes. Then there were George and Eliot, they were twins. Then, Sheldon Gold, briefly.

RANDY: How many did you sleep with?

FRANCIS: Sleep with? They didn't even talk to me.

RANDY: You never told them how you felt?

FRANCIS: Well, that's it, you see. I'm never sure how I feel, really.

RANDY: Have you ever had sex with a man? (*Francis shakes his head "no"*)

Were there girls before Judith?

FRANCIS: Well, there was Elaine Hoffenburg. She had braces.

RANDY: Braces on her teeth?

FRANCIS: Legs. I took her to the Senior Prom.

(*Randy looks incredulous*)

Well, I was no catch, either. I was very fat then. It wasn't too bad. Once she got enough momentum going, she could do a passable waltz. Then there was Luise Morely. Slightly pockmarked but pretty in a plain sort of way. We held hands through *The Sandpiper,* then we did it afterwards. It was my first time. Elaine had been willing, but it was a little hard getting her legs apart.

RANDY: Gross! I worked for months to get Nancy Simmons to go to the prom with me, then I got car sick on the way and threw up all over her; and you remember Roberta Hasserfluth, I broke up with her just as you and Judith got together, well, we decided we would do it, so we went to the drive in movie in Waltham. It was *The Four Stewardesses*—

FRANCIS: Wasn't that in 3-D?

RANDY: Oh, was it ever, we had to wear goggles and everything. Well, I bought this bottle of Mateus, see, and since I'd never bought wine before I forgot you needed a corkscrew. So I couldn't get it open, so there we are watching this dirty movie in the dead of winter, with this bottle of Mateus between my legs, trying to get it open with my car key—

FRANCIS: Well, did you ever do it?

RANDY: Too cold! I'm sort of a jerk with girls, but I like them. I like you too, you're my friend. But I don't think I'm in love with you. Does that mean you were in love with me?

(*Francis shrugs*)

I mean, Francis, has it ever occurred to you you might be suffering from homosexual panic.

FRANCIS: (*Snaps his fingers*) I knew I should have taken Psych. 101.

RANDY: I mean, it's true. It's really common in a competitive society.

FRANCIS: (*Shakes his head, irritated at being put on*) Oh, really.

RANDY: I'm serious. I mean, if you've never slept with a man, never laid a hand on me . . .

FRANCIS: Are you saying that if you were to strip right now and lie down inside that tent, I couldn't—well, do anything?

RANDY: Well, there's only one way to find out.
(*Starts to strip*)

FRANCIS: What are you doing? Randy, what are you doing?

RANDY: I'm stripping.

FRANCIS: Are you crazy? In front of me? Here?
(*Francis makes a dash for his door, but Randy intercepts him. Randy stands in front of the door, blocking it. He looks around the yard, up at the windows, then unzips his fly*)
Jesus Christ!

RANDY: (*Walks over to the tent*) I'll save the rest for inside the tent.
(*Crawls inside*)

FRANCIS: Jesus Christ! Oh Jesus . . .
(*Holding his chin*)
I didn't shave this morning.
(*Francis is about to crawl into the tent, as Herschel comes bounding in from the alley*)

HERSCHEL: How's Randy?

FRANCIS: (*Exasperated*) Jesus Christ, Herschel, he's dead!

HERSCHEL: (*Horror struck*) He is??!!

FRANCIS: Ten minutes ago; heart failure.

HERSCHEL: Are you sure? I mean, I faked a heart attack in gym class last month. Maybe he's faking. Call an ambulance!

FRANCIS: Damn it, Herschel, he's dead, now go away!

HERSCHEL: Can I see the body?

RANDY: (*Sticks his head out of the tent*) Hello, Herschel.

HERSCHEL: Randy! He said . . .

RANDY: I heard. Look, Herschel, Francis and I . . .

FRANCIS: (*Trying to stop him*) Randy!

RANDY: . . . are involved in a very serious ritual. We will both be drummed out of our exclusive clubs at Harvard if we don't do this.

HERSCHEL: Oh, heavy.

RANDY: Very. So Herschel, would you please go away and come back a little later?

HERSCHEL: Sure.

(*He sets a little bottle of Tylenol in front of the tent, and starts for the alley. Randy throws the shorts out at Francis. Herschel turns back*)

Like five minutes?

FRANCIS: (*Grabs the shorts, hides them behind his back*) Herschel, take a long walk!

(*Herschel, dejected, exits out the alley. Francis hesitates, peers into the tent, and finally crawls inside. There is no movement for a few seconds, then Randy, wrapped in the sleeping bag, comes bounding out of the tent, followed by Francis*) Randy, what's the matter? What's the matter? Why did you strip if you didn't mean it? Were you bringing me on?

RANDY: No!

(*Runs back into the tent*)

FRANCIS: Is that what was going on this spring? Perhaps somewhere in some subconscious avenue of that boy-man mind of yours you sensed I had a vulnerable point and decided to make the most of it?

RANDY: (*From inside the tent*) I was seventeen fucking years old this spring—what's your excuse?

FRANCIS: Well, you're eighteen now.

RANDY: (*Coming out of tent, wearing jeans*) I liked you!

FRANCIS: (*Sarcastic*) Thanks!

RANDY: I really did.

FRANCIS: It's vicious of you.

RANDY: How?

FRANCIS: Because you did it all just to humiliate me—

RANDY: I really do like you. I mean, liking does exist, doesn't it? It doesn't have to include sex, or love, or deep need, does it?

FRANCIS: I don't know.

RANDY: I don't know either.

FRANCIS: I don't know either.

RANDY: Boy . . . you are really fucked up.
(*He embraces Francis*)

FRANCIS: I know.

(*He puts his arms around Randy. Judith enters the yard from the gate carrying a large gaily wrapped box. She sees this embrace and lets out a surprised yell. The two jump apart, confused, and looking guilty*)

RANDY: Judith!

JUDITH: You're disgusting!

RANDY: It's not my fault, he's older than I am!

JUDITH: He's younger than you are!

FRANCIS: Judith . . .

JUDITH: (*Turns on him*) And you!

FRANCIS: Now, look, Judith, it didn't have anything to do with sex!

JUDITH: Oh, no! I'm sure! Nothing you do has anything to do with sex! It's all a bring on, isn't it? You get to that point, and then, you're ugly, or you're fat, or you're gay! What did you use on him? That you were ugly, fat, and straight? Well, I'm on to you! Happy birthday!

(*She throws the box at Francis*)

FRANCIS: Act your age Judith!

JUDITH: Oh ho, act my age, act my age says this paragon of maturity, this pristine sage now come of age!

FRANCIS: It's hard to explain . . .

RANDY: That's right!

JUDITH: Hard? Hard to explain? What is? You're going to fuck my brother, that's very simple, that's the birds and the bees, that's Biology 1A. I thought I loved you. I thought I loved you!

(*Starts hitting Randy*)
I thought I loved him!

FRANCIS: Judith, will you please calm down.

JUDITH: And my mother told me never to trust fatties, they're self-indulgent. Go have a banana split!

RANDY: For Christ' sake, calm down!

JUDITH: I knew there was something suspicious in your wanting to come along. I bet the two of you were laughing at me, comparing notes, carrying on behind my back the whole time. Why, Francis, why would you do this to me?

FRANCIS: He was bringing me on, standing here with no clothes on, hanging onto me, what would you do?

JUDITH: Puke!

RANDY: Do you think I enjoyed it? Huh, tubby?

JUDITH: (*To Randy*) So you're a faggot too—won't the sophomore class be surprised?

RANDY: Why are you screaming at me, it's his fault!

FRANCIS: (*Shaking his finger at Randy*) It's your fault!

JUDITH: Oh, my God, it's love! M and M—mutual masturbation!

RANDY: (*Angry*) I thought I could help him, I should have known better, I can't help you— (*Shoves Francis. Herschel comes bounding in from alley*)

HERSCHEL: Randy, your ceremony seems to be over, we can go see the . . .

RANDY: (*Screaming, runs into tent*) And I can't help you either, Herschel!

HERSCHEL: Francis . . .

FRANCIS: God damn it, Herschel, go away!

HERSCHEL: Oh, no, I did it again!
(*Judith is on one side of the stage, talking to Francis, and Herschel is on the other side, talking to the tent*)

JUDITH: And I was even out buying you a present!

HERSCHEL: I tried to be your friend, I don't know how . . .

JUDITH: And I was willing to be understanding.

HERSCHEL: I'm just stupid.

JUDITH: All those Callas records, and I hate her voice and her wobble!

FRANCIS: She only wobbles on the late recordings!

HERSCHEL: What did I do?!

JUDITH: And that Toti dal Monte, for Christ' sake, she sounds like a broken steam engine!

FRANCIS: Her mad scene is still the best on records!

HERSCHEL: It's just me!

JUDITH: And what about my mad scene?

HERSCHEL: I'm just retarded like they all say!

(*He runs into his house*)

RANDY: (*From inside the tent*) Shut up Judith!

JUDITH: Oh God, and I even came here bringing your beloved! And you kissed me, and you stroked me, and we held hands along the Charles River, and I thought: He's weird, he's pudgy, he likes Maria Callas, but he responds to me! What a laugh! That's funnier than *The Barber of Seville*, that's funnier than *The Girl of the Golden West*—

FRANCIS: Shut up, shut up, Judith, God damn it, act your age! You're like a fucking six-year-old!

JUDITH: And you? How old are you?!

(*They are right in front of the Geminiani door. Bunny, Fran, and Lucille enter grandly from Fran's house, carrying a huge birthday cake and singing. They are wearing party hats. Bunny is running around, putting hats on Judith and Francis, and Randy, as he emerges from the tent. Fran has the cake on the same typing table that was used for breakfast. He also has a camera*)

BUNNY, FRAN AND LUCILLE:

"Happy birthday to you,
Happy birthday to you,
Happy birthday, dear Francis,
Happy birthday to you!"

FRAN: Happy birthday, my son!

(*Snaps a picture*)

LUCILLE: Come on, blow out the candles and cut the cake, it's too hot to wait.

BUNNY: There's only six candles, all we could find.

(*Francis is about to blow them out*)

LUCILLE: Come on, make a wish.

(*He does. Fran takes another picture, and Francis blows out the candles. They all cheer and applaud. Judith and Randy are still stunned*)

FRANCIS: Thank you. I would first like to thank my father, now that I am officially an adult, for teaching me how to dance and sing and cough and fart and scratch and above all how to treat a rash once it becomes visible to the general public, then I would like to thank my next-door neighbor Bunny . . .

(*Fran snaps a photo of Bunny*)

for demonstrating once and for all that motherhood ought to be abolished, along with drunks and whores, Lucille, for teaching me how to ruin the happiest occasion with one glance and the cheapest insect spray, and Randy, for providing us with living proof of the vacuity of American Higher Education, and then Judith, our brilliant, bubbly, and let's not forget, mature Italian major from Radcliffe will recite to us in her main-line Italian all the nonsense syllables of her upbringing and her recent reading. And I want you all to know precisely what I think of all this: this neighborhood, Bunny and Lucille, Randy and Judith!

(*He rips into the cake with his hands and tears it apart, hurling pieces at Judith and the others. All duck away. After Francis has destroyed the cake, he runs off through the gate. Herschel stumbles out of his house, holding the bag of rat poison, powder all over his mouth*)

HERSCHEL: I swallowed Uncle Eddie's rat poison!

BUNNY: My baby!

FRAN: Holy shit!

BUNNY: (*On her knees by Herschel*) My baby!

LUCILLE: Who's gonna clean it up, hanh?

BLACKOUT

SCENE 2

Evening. Fran has a huge trash bag and is cleaning up the yard. Lucille is sitting on the divider between the two houses. Randy is finished packing. Their tent has been struck and is rolled up again.

LUCILLE: Rum and chocolate sauce everywhere—did he know how much it cost?

FRAN: Well, it was his birthday cake, if he wanted a throw it around, it's his right I guess.

LUCILLE: But it ain't his right to clean it up, hanh?

(*She points to a piece of cake*)

Over there. Jesus, I'm sick and tired of cleanin' up afta people.

(*Points again*)

Over here. Cleanin' up afta my brothers . . .

FRAN: (*Under his breath, still picking up*)

Your brothers . . .

LUCILLE: Afta pop . . .

FRAN: Afta pop . . .

LUCILLE: Then my mom got senile . . .

FRAN: Then mom . . .

LUCILLE: Then my husband . . .

FRAN: Your husband . . .

LUCILLE: Then Donny . . .

FRAN: (*Joking*) Ain't he at Yale?

LUCILLE: Hanh? Of course he's at Yale, that's a stupid question, *ma stupidezza* . . .

RANDY: I'll see if Judith is ready.

(*Runs into Bunny's house*)

FRAN: I hope Francis gets back soon—I think his guests are gonna leave any minute—

LUCILLE: Well, I'm surprised they stayed as long as they did. Well, at least he didn't play so much opera music this weekend—all that screamin'—that's what I got against opera, Fran, ain't like real life.

(*She tries to clean up some whipped cream with a Kleenex. Bunny enters from her house, depressed*)

BUNNY: Yo, Fran.

FRAN: Yo, Bun. How's Herschel?

BUNNY: Better and better, just ate all my leftovers.

FRAN: I guess they're gettin' ready to leave.

BUNNY: Yep.

LUCILLE: (*About Bunny, mean*) *E questa si chiama una madre?*

FRAN: Lucille, take this bag in the house—tape up the top so nothin' gets in . . .

(*Lucille takes the bag, and goes into Fran's house. He calls after her*)

And put on the coffee!

BUNNY: (*Sits down on her stoop*) She could use a enema, lye and hot pepper!

(*Looks at Fran*)

Remember way back when, when we did it?

FRAN: Oh, Bun.

BUNNY: Oh, Fran! 'Sbeen a long time. I think it's time we did it again. Don't say it, you got Lucille! What's Lucille? Shit, she gotta get on the subway to get her hips movin'.

FRAN: You don' need me, Bun.

BUNNY: We was good together.

FRAN: How often? Five times the most? I remember the first time. (*He sits down beside her*)

You remember? We forced Francis to take Herschel to the movies; it was *Lady and the Tramp*. They was that young, we could force them. Can you see the two of them together?

BUNNY: They was both so fat they probably took up a whole row between them.

FRAN: Didn't they have rashes too?

BUNNY: Nah, that was the third time. We forced Francis to take Herschel into Center City to buy calamine lotion.

(*She puts her head on his shoulder. He looks up to his window, checking for Lucille*)

FRAN: Why don't you give Sam a call?

BUNNY: He ain't interested.

FRAN: I bet you still like him.

BUNNY: You still like your wife?

FRAN: Sure, I married her, didn't I? We went together two years and were pretty happy until Francis came along. She wasn't the same after that. Oh well, she's gone. And now there's Lucille—at least she bakes good fiadone. And she's good people, even if she schives too much. I mean, what kinda choice I got? Hanh? Women today, they look at you, they see a man wheezin', coughin', goin' to the bathroom, scratchin', gettin' rashes, they take off. But Sam ain't attached yet—give him a call, fix yourself up, grow up a little—

BUNNY: Grow up a little? Like that was easy. Jesus, if only I didn't still act and feel nineteen. I look in the mirror and I know there's fat and wrinkles there, Jesus Christ do I know there's fat and wrinkles! Yet, I'll be damned if I don't still, somewhere in there, see this nineteen-year-old filly hot to trot and on fire for some kind of success in life!

(*Looks at house, tricycle*)

And look what I got—

FRAN: So Herschel's a little crazy, but he's gonna do wonders—

BUNNY: He's a fuckin' genius! Grow up a little. And what about Francis?

FRAN: Don't know, this Judith girl—

BUNNY: She seems to like him, hard as that is to believe, but I don't see much evidence of his liking her.

FRAN: No, I guess not, but kids nowadays, maybe they act different when they're goin' together—and maybe she isn't his last chance.

BUNNY: Don't kid yourself. Look, why don't you just ask him and save yourself years of wonderin' and never bein' sure . . . ?

FRAN: It's the hardest thing for a father to ask his son. Don' know why it should be, I know guys who . . . like . . . other guys who are regular, you know, in every other way. But you know, it's his life now, he's gonna pay the consequences for whatever he does . . . but still, I hope.

BUNNY: Well, I worry about Herschel too. But Jesus, I figure we're lucky if he lives to be twenty-one—

LUCILLE: (*Appears in the doorway*) Yo, Fran!

FRAN: (*Gets away from Bunny*) Yo, Lucille!

LUCILLE: I see the monster comin' down the street— (*She goes back in*)

FRAN: Bunny, let's go inside, he won't want to see us right off—
(*They go into Bunny's house. Francis enters from the gate. He sees the packed knapsacks under the fig tree. After a moment, Judith enters from Bunny's house. She is wearing a skirt and blouse*)

JUDITH: Well . . . Azael has returned.

FRANCIS: Who?

JUDITH: Who else? The Prodigal!
(*Lucille comes out of Fran's house, carrying a coffee pot, and a new robe for Herschel. She sees Francis*)

LUCILLE: *Ma Sporcacione!* (*She slams the door, and goes into Bunny's house*)

FRANCIS: Is everyone furious at me?

JUDITH: We have Bunny's uncle on the force waiting inside with handcuffs.

FRANCIS: Oh Jesus, you're at it again—

JUDITH: Well, to be serious, Lucille is making a novena to Saint Jude the Obscure, Patron Saint of the Hopeless and Pudgy who spoil their own birthday parties.

(She gets a sweater out of her knapsack)
Herschel took rat poison.

FRANCIS: Is he dead?

JUDITH: No more than ever. Bunny called her uncle on the ambulance squad and he was rushed to St. Agnes Hospital, across Track 37 on the A, the AA 1 through 7, and the B express lines, perhaps you've passed it? They cleaned up the yard as best they could, but you'll probably be finding birthday cake here and there for the next few months. Still the fall rains and the march of time should wash away all stains from your yard, your life, and these, the Days of our Youth! Thank you.

FRANCIS: And you're leaving.

JUDITH: You noticed! Maybe you aren't autistic. Yes, we're walking over to Broad Street, where we will get a cab to 30th Street Station, where we will take the 9:05 train to Boston, from there we're going to our summer home. We are not hitching, you'll notice, we've lost the stomach for it. Oh, by the way, happy birthday.

FRANCIS: Thank you.

JUDITH: I'm sorry.

FRANCIS: So am I.

(They are about to go to each other, when Randy comes out of Bunny's house)

RANDY: C'mon Judith. We have nineteen minutes to catch that train.

(Fran and Lucille come out of Bunny's house)

FRAN: So, Igor's back, hanh? I guess you kids is off.

(Randy and Judith are putting on their knapsacks and collecting their belongings)

RANDY: We're off!

LUCILLE: Goodbye!

FRAN: The way I see it, life is made up of hellos and goodbyes and forgivin' and forgettin'. So you two forgive and forget and come back, hanh? Even if Frankenstein ain't here, you're always welcome.

(Bunny comes out of her house with Herschel. He is wearing clean pajamas and a new bathrobe)

BUNNY: (*Sees Francis*) So, Igor's back, hanh?

(*To Randy and Judith*) We wanted to see youse off, you're good people, you kids.

LUCILLE: (*To Judith*) If I give you Donny's number at Yale maybe you could get in touch with him this fall, he's nice, real good looking and athletic, and he ain't no party pooper neither.

(*She gives Judith a slip of paper*)

I have somethin' in the house for you.

(*She goes inside*)

HERSCHEL: (*To Randy, shyly*) Like, if I promise to lose weight and get less weird, can we be friends?

RANDY: Sure, even if you gain and get weirder.

HERSCHEL: Like, don't lie to me, you know? Like, I understand if you aren't interested. But can I like, you know, write you letters?

RANDY: Oh sure. I'll give you our summer address, otherwise, just write me at Harvard.

(*He writes address on a little piece of paper that Herschel had ready. Lucille returns with a plate wrapped in tin foil. The following three lines, are said at about the same time*)

JUDITH: C'mon Randy, let's go!

LUCILLE: C'mon Randy, you're gonna miss the train.

RANDY: See you, Herschel.

(*Judith, Fran, and Lucille go out through the gate. They stand in the entrance saying final goodbyes. Randy, about to say goodbye to Francis, is grabbed by Bunny*)

BUNNY: Oh, honey bun, I feel like I've known you for years. Maybe I'm gettin' funny in the head, but I know a promising hunk when I see one.

RANDY: Thank you.

BUNNY: I'm gonna miss you.

(*Randy smiles and tries to get away but she hangs on*)

JUDITH: (*Calling from the gate*) C'mon Randy!

BUNNY: Be careful when you sit down on toilets, put paper there, you hear? And see that some people may be pretty, even if they got strange faces, and mean well, even if they act weird, and think of me once in a while, hanh?

(*She kisses him*)

Goodbye!

(*She goes into her house. Herschel and Randy shake hands, then Herschel, looking back sadly, blinking back tears, follows his mother into the house*)

RANDY: (*Goes to Francis*) In the fall, right?

FRANCIS: Right.

(*They shake hands*)

JUDITH: Randy!

RANDY: Listen, I was just trying to help, okay?

(*Randy leaves. The goodbyes are heard from behind the fence. Francis is left alone*)

FRAN: Come back soon! Please!

(*Francis goes into his room, and puts on a quiet, sad piece of music. Fran and Lucille come back into the yard*)

Let's go to your place, hanh? Need some coffee.

LUCILLE: I got some nice cheese cake for you, Fran.

FRAN: Yeah? Sounds good.

(*Yells to Francis*)

Yo, Francis! We're goin' a Lucille's for coffee and cake. Wanna come?

(*There is no answer*) Yo, Francis!

FRANCIS: (*From his room*) God damn it, no!

FRAN: That's my Ivy League son.

(*Fran and Lucille exit through the gate. Francis appears in his window. He is very agitated. The music is playing*)

FRANCIS: Jesus Christ, what am I doing?

(*Calls out*)

Dad! Dad! Yo Dad!

(*He runs out of the house, to the gate*)

FRAN: (*Heard from offstage*) What is it?

FRANCIS: Give me some coin, I'm going to Boston! (*Runs back into his room*)

FRAN: (*Running into yard*) Jesus Christ in Heaven! Yo, Bun!
(*Bunny's lights go on. Francis turns off the music*)

BUNNY: (*At her window*) Yo, Fran!

FRAN: Call your uncle on the ambulance service. We gotta get Francis to the train!

BUNNY: Holy shit!
(*She goes to her telephone in the kitchen*)

LUCILLE: (*Running into house*) I'll help you pack.

BUNNY: (*On the phone*) Hello, Uncle Marty, bring your fuckin' ambulance down, we gotta make a train!

HERSCHEL: (*Coming out of his house*) What's going on?

FRAN: Francis is going to Boston.

HERSCHEL: To see Randy?

BUNNY: (*Still on the phone*) Hello, Uncle Jimmy, send a fuckin' squad car down, we gotta make a train.

FRAN: Hey, Herschel! Catch them kids.
(*Pushes him to the gate*)

HERSCHEL: This way's quicker!
(*Runs out through alley behind his house*)

FRAN: (*Yelling after him*) And bring them back! I'm fuckin' outta money. Lucille!

LUCILLE: (*In Francis' room, with a large laundry bag*) There ain't no clean clothes in here!

FRAN: You got some money, I'm out.

LUCILLE: (*Hurling coin purse out the window*) Look!

FRANCIS: Oh, I want to take my new records—Callas in *Parsifal*, 1950, and the 1955 *Norma!*
(*Runs into his room*)

FRAN: (*Going through change purse*) Jesus Christ, Lucille, all these pennies!

LUCILLE: For the tax!

FRAN: Yo, Bun!

BUNNY: Yo, Fran!

FRAN: We need some more money!

(*Bunny comes out of her house, reaches into her bosom, and removes wad*)

BUNNY: Here's the house money, take what you need.

(*Sirens are heard in the distance, getting closer*)

They're comin'!

(*Francis runs out of the house, holding record albums*)

You stick wit me, kid, I got connections!

(*Hugs Francis, as Fran counts money*) Where's Gargantua?

FRAN: He went to get the kids.

(*To Francis*)

I think this is enough—

(*Gives him money*)

BUNNY: I hope he doesn't frighten them away!

LUCILLE: (*Runs out of the house with the laundry bag*) This is the best I could do—go to a laundromat when you get there!

(*Francis takes bag, hugs her*)

FRANCIS: Thanks everybody, I mean, thanks . . .

FRAN: Well, it's your birthday.

(*Sirens increase. Herschel comes running in from the alley with Judith and Randy*)

HERSCHEL: I got 'em! I got 'em!

FRAN: They're back!

(*Francis embraces Judith. Sirens much louder*)

BUNNY: (*At gate*) My uncles is here!

(*The kids run out. The others watch at the gate*)

FRAN: (*Checks his watch, then puts his arms around Lucille and Bunny*) I think they're gonna make it!

BLACKOUT

The Transfiguration
of Benno Blimpie

The stage is divided as follows:

BENNO'S ROOM

Benno, an enormously fat young man of twenty, sits on a stool from which he can survey the action comfortably. This is in an area somewhat removed from the rest of the stage. The area represents Benno's current room, in which he has barricaded himself. He sits on his stool for the entire length of the play.

When Benno is involved in a scene he acts as if he were present, and the others act the same. In these scenes he is playing a young boy, and he makes this plain by changing his voice slightly so that it is higher.

His clothes are very large on him, and tent-like. They look as if they haven't been washed or changed in weeks. His complexion is blotchy and pockmarked. His hair is greasy and full of tangles.

THE PARK

This is another area, where trash and dead leaves are scattered about. It is inhabited by the Girl and the Old Man—all their scenes take place here.

The Old Man is Benno's grandfather, an Italian immigrant, about seventy. The Girl is from the neighborhood, thirteen, tough, Irish parents.

THE KITCHEN

A third area, this represents the kitchen in the home of Benno's parents, and of the young Benno. Once again, this is an area somewhat isolated, and it should reflect an urban working-class home.

Benno's parents are seen as they were when he was a young boy. His father is in his early thirties or very late twenties, good looking, a former athlete. His mother is older than the father, less attractive.

It should be kept in mind that Benno is remembering the scenes that are acted out on stage. Thus he is controlling them. He watches these scenes with great intensity and concentration.

The Transfiguration of Benno Blimpie was first presented at the Eugene O'Neill Memorial Theatre Center and later performed Off Off Broadway at the Ensemble Studio Theatre and the Direct Theatre. It was produced by Adela Holzer at the Astor Place Theatre, New York City, opening March 10, 1977. The direction was by Robert Drivas, the sets and costumes by Rubén de Saavedra, and the lighting by Ian Calderon. The cast, in order of appearance, was as follows:

Benno	JAMES COCO
Old Man	PETER CAREW
Mother	ROSEMARY de ANGELIS
Girl	K. McKENNA
Father	ROGER SERBAGI

SCENE ONE

Lights up on Benno, eating.

In dim light, one by one, Mother, Father, Girl, Old Man in characteristic poses.

They freeze. Benno finishes eating and speaks to the audience.

BENNO: I am Benno. I am eating myself to death.

BLACKOUT

SCENE TWO

Lights up on Benno. He speaks to the audience.

BENNO: And there were weeds, feet and bugs. There were black ants and red ants and giant ants and worms. There were worms and spiders and snails. One day I crushed one hundred eighteen snails with my bare feet. I was very fat even then. It was after a rain storm. I ran in the grass and took off my shoes and socks. The snails inched out and I smashed everyone I saw for an hour. I had snail blood all over my feet. My grandfather asked me what it was.

OLD MAN: (*The Park. He speaks as though Benno were a little boy standing beside him*) Eh, Benno, what you got all over you feet, hanh? You mother gonna give me hell. Why can't you look afta yourself, hanh? What is that shit on you feet?

BENNO: (*High voice, playing little boy, acting as though he were beside the Old Man*) Snail wine.

OLD MAN: You crazy, crazy!

(*Hits where Benno would be standing. Benno reacts to the blow in place. The lights go down on the Old Man, but stay up on Benno. Ice cream truck jingle heard*)

BENNO: I have eaten seventeen chocolate cones today. Soft ice cream, the kind they sell in trucks. Those trucks announce themselves with tinkling, mechanical tunes played over and over. I heard the neighborhood truck making its rounds and I ran out and bought seventeen cones. Chocolate. I was out of breath from running down the stairs.

(*A light up on Benno's mother in kitchen. Benno changes his voice to a high whine. Mother reacts as though he were beside her and busies herself in the kitchen. Benno, high voice*)

Momma, I wanna chocolate cone.

MOTHER: You're too fat as it is, Benno.

BENNO: I'm hungry. I wanna chocolate cone.

MOTHER: Shut up, fatsy. Why are you so fat? Tell me that. Hanh? Why are you so fat? Well, at least fat men got big ones.

BENNO: Ma, I want one.

MOTHER: I remember old Joey Fercanti around the corner in the old neighborhood. We was growin' up together. He was fatter even than you. He took my sister and me inna the alley one day and took it out and stuffed it inna his shirt pocket. He said: God provides for fat guys. An' I turned him down. I hadda go out an' marry that father of yours, the bastid. Joey was a looker even if he was fat. Better than you, God knows. Not all them blotches in the face and he didn't fall down every ten minutes. Well . . . maybe God'll give you a big one, but sure as hell, I doubt it.

BENNO: Ma, please, I want one.

MOTHER: Shut your face, fat jerk!

(*Lights dim out on Mother*)

BENNO: (*To audience*) Mother. I used to think my father dropped roaches down her slit and that's why I heard her high giggle at night. There was no door between their room and mine; just a curtain with a rip in it. I heard her high giggle and I thought my father must have collected a lot of cockroaches that night in the cellar and was dropping them down her drain. A lot of them twisting in her tubes; suffocating, fornicating, giving birth; you know, whatever cockroaches do in cunts. And when she went into the bathroom and washed afterwards, you see, I thought she was flooding them out and down the toilet. Then one night I watched through the rip in the curtain. I preferred the cockroaches. Father.

(*Father enters tossing a football*)

FATHER: And now, playing center quarterback and primary receiver for Bishop Neumann, Number 64, Dominick Vertucci!

(*He plays wildly, pantomiming a frenzied football game. He plays as though he were the star of the team and is driving them to victory. He pantomimes hearing cheers for himself and raises his hands over his head in victory*)

Geez, geez, thanks, I couldna done it without the guys—thanks, geez . . .

(*Catches himself, becomes flustered and shamefaced*)

Aw, shit, was only pretendin' Benno. Even I pretend sometimes. Gotta go home anyways. You bitch mother raise hell if we're late. Come on, Benno.

(*Leaves sadly. As though taking Benno's hand*)

Don't trip over this curb . . . (*Benno trips*)

Aw shit, Benno!

(*Father exits. Lights come up on the Park. The Girl plays. Out of the corner of her eye she watches the Old Man who watches her intently. She allows her game to take her close to him*)

GIRL: (*To the Old Man*) Hey you! Buy me a chocolate cone.

OLD MAN: You mother, what she say?

GIRL: Who's gonna tell her?

(*A pause. She plays her game again*)

OLD MAN: I seen you. I seen you playin' in the street. You tough. How old?

GIRL: Buy me a cone.

OLD MAN: Can't. My Social Security check ain't come this month. Down to my last dime.

GIRL: The man'll trust you. C'mon. Buy me a chocolate cone.

(*A pause*)

OLD MAN: Come on. Benno, come on.

(*They walk off hand in hand*)

BENNO: I was in an oven. A fat roast burning in the oven. There was a glass door to my oven and they came to it and laughed and pointed. Fat roasts are funny burning in ovens. I couldn't move. If I moved, I burned my back. If I moved I burned my side. If I turned, old burns were given to the heat. I was trapped, you see. Once I thought, wait until you're older, Benno, wait until you're older. Strength then, and force enough to burst through the oven door into the sun, into freedom. One day I did break through the glass door. But on the other side all there was was another oven with another glass door and laughing people pointing at me. And there was no sun. Has there ever been a sun? I am still in the oven, I am still in the oven, I am still in the oven. And I am burning up, trapped and pierced, burning up! That's why I am eating myself to death.

BLACKOUT

SCENE THREE

Lights up on the Park and on Benno. Benno has a flashlight with which he plays for a moment before the scene begins.

The Park is lit to suggest a very shady area of the park. The light fades into heavy darkness.

The Girl enters barefoot. She walks slowly through the mud, humming to herself, occasionally she stops and wanders a step or two backwards.

Very slowly, the Old Man enters. He is obviously following her, and has been. The Girl realizes this but doesn't show it. As she approaches the dark area she stops and plays in place. He watches her rapt for a moment, then decides to speak.

Benno pays intense attention to the scene.

OLD MAN: What you doin' playin' inna mud?

GIRL: Walkin' barefoot.

OLD MAN: Dummy, you cut you feet.

GIRL: I want it.

OLD MAN: There are snakes and rats in here. They eat little girls, startin' down there. And swallow them, whole. Be careful.

GIRL: Ain't a little girl. An' I want to.

OLD MAN: You wanna cut you feet?

GIRL: I dunno.

(*A pause. She walks a bit toward the dark area*) Maybe a man'll come by and pick the glass outta the cut. Maybe a man'll hold my foot and lick it and cry over it.

OLD MAN: You're crazy!

(*A pause*)

Men hide around here. Under them heavy trees. They hide, you hear? And they wait. For little girls to come by, barefoot. Little girls don't fight hard. (*A pause*) Little girls, they got soft feet. Men wait with rope, to tie them, hard. Be careful!

GIRL: (*After a moment*) Take your shoes and socks off.

OLD MAN: What? Why?

GIRL: I want it. C'mon. Walk with me. Over here, in the shade, under these trees.

(*She walks into the dark area and vanishes. The Old Man waits an instant, then takes his shoes and socks off. The socks are white with a pronounced yellow tinge. He walks in after the Girl. Benno has watched and listened to this scene intently. The light brightens on him. He shines his flashlight around the area the Old Man and Girl have just left—the area which isn't dark. Then shines the flashlight into his own eyes. He squints and shudders*)

BENNO: (*Quickly, passionately*) Cimabue, Giotto, Donatello, Pico Della Mirandola, Bellini, Michelangelo, Rafaello, Botticelli, Brunelleschi, I want, I want, want, want, want, Brunelleschi, Botticelli, Rafaello, Michelangelo, Bellini, Pico Della Mirandola, Donatello, Giotto, Cimabue. I want, please, please, I want—wantwantwantwantwantwant! Give me . . . give me . . .
(*He is panting, his eyes are shut tightly. He has begun to cry*)
No one, no one, no one . . . no . . . one . . .
(*He shines the flashlight slowly into the dark area. The Old Man is caressing and kissing the Girl's feet. She moans. Hold a moment*)

BLACKOUT

SCENE FOUR

Lights up on the Kitchen, and on Benno.

Benno doesn't change positions, but takes part intently in the scene. The Mother and Father act as though he were present. They talk to him as though he were sitting in the third place set at the table. Benno uses his high voice.

MOTHER: (*To the Father*) Eh, Dominick! Where's your old man?
FATHER: How the hell should I know?
MOTHER: He's your father!
(*She busies herself. The Father consults a racing sheet with great interest. He has a pencil in hand and figures numbers along the side of the sheet. After a while, the Mother glares at him*) Look! What is your father, the star boarder? Hanh? Tell me that, what is your father? I tell him and tell him we have supper at six on the dot and does he show? Hanh? Hanh? He don't show. What am I supposed to do with the food—Benno, don't smack your lips like a pig, PIG! Oink, oink, oink!—leave it out for the rats? I asked you, Dominick, what am I supposed to do with the food?
(*The Father ignores her*)

That's right, Mary, slave for them and let them ignore you. Gotta cook twice, gotta clean up twice, and I work too. What is this, a hotel? Hanh? Your no good, free-loadin' father come up to the table afta we finish, like a big rat!

FATHER: Look, fry the steak, I'm hungry. And I want it rare.

MOTHER: Awwww! Eat it raw, you creep!

FATHER: I wanna see the blood. That's how you know it's rare, you can see the blood.

BENNO: (*High voice. Trying to make friends with his father*) That's how you know it's rare, you can see the blood.

MOTHER: (*To Benno*) You shut up, fatty. What the hell do you know? (*To the Father*) Looka him bustin' outta those pants and looka those blotches on his face. He's enough to break mirrors, God forbid! And don't get me off the topic of the star boarder. T'resa was sayin' . . .

FATHER: You got red peppers in them potatoes?

MOTHER: We run out.

FATHER: (*Suddenly angry*) God damn it to hell, you know I want red peppers in the fried potatoes! That's when they're good. They burn when they go down.

BENNO: (*As before*) They burn when they go down.

MOTHER: (*To Benno*) Shut up, you fat creep! (*To the Father*) And you! Who the hell are you to start screaming at me like you own the place? Hanh? What the hell are you? Nothin', that's what! Up to your ass in debt, a lousy gambler. Who works their ass off? Who slaves? I do—Mary, that's who. I get up and work myself to the bone for you and your monster kid and your free-loading old man. I go to work at six and then have to come home to look after you and this disgraziato freak! How much did you give me for the house last week, hanh? Tell me that, big man, big horse player, how much did you give me for the house? A big fat fifteen dollars, that's how much! That's supposed to pay the mortgage, buy food, pay this cripple's doctor bills and keep your no good, smelly father in stogies! How far's fifteen dollars supposed to go, hanh? What's it supposed to buy—the Taj Mahal? You wanna good meal, you go to the bookie, go to the Pooch! You love him more than you love me!

FATHER: (*Retreating behind the racing form*) All right, all right.

MOTHER: You was always out bettin' them nags. This nag, this nag, Mary, you never bet on. You want red pepper! Who the hell are you to want red pepper? You can't even get it up.

FATHER: You stupid bitch! In front of the kid!

MOTHER: Kid? What kid? Where's the kid? You ever see a kid that looked like that? He's just like you—nothin'. A ton of nothin'!

FATHER: (*Angry again*) Whose fault? Hanh? Whose fault? Without red pepper he can't digest. Red peppers eat up the fat. You eat red peppers, you can eat anything, even the shit you cook and still stay thin and healthy. The shit you cook! How do you cook it, hanh? By sittin' on it? It smells of your ass! It smells of your friggin' cunt!

MOTHER: How would you know? You ain't been in it for years— all you smell is the Pooch!

FATHER: And another thing, you friggin' Napolitan bitch, you never, never put enough oregano in the gravy. And you never put enough oil. It's dry, like your tits! Not enough red pepper, not enough oregano, not enough oil, no wonder you got a freak for a son! That's why he ain't normal!

MOTHER: He ain't normal because he takes after you! He got no balls either. Your father is ball-less, you is ball-less. And your kid is ball-less. It runs in the family. I looked at him last night. There ain't nothin' down there, only flab. And your father's screwin' a thirteen-year-old girl. Everybody knows.

FATHER: You shut that big, ugly Napolitan mouth!

MOTHER: Madonna me'! The whole neighborhood knows. Your father's a sex fiend and he's livin' in my house. And she's a Irish girl, the slut, the putana!

FATHER: Shut up! Shut up!

MOTHER: (*Screaming*) Your father's a bum, you're a ball-less bum with no cock and your son's a good-for-nothin' ball-less bum!

FATHER: Cunt!

(*He slaps her. She throws herself to the floor as though the blow had sent her reeling*)

BENNO: (*High voice*) Daddy!

MOTHER: (*On the floor, hysterical*) That's right! Run off to the Pooch! You love him more than you ever loved me!

BENNO: (*High voice, crying*) Mommy!

MOTHER: Get away from me, you good-for-nothin' fatty you! You louse, you good-for-nothin'—you—fruit!

(*Crawls off, weeping*)

BENNO: My steak is rare, I can see the blood.

BLACKOUT

SCENE FIVE

Lights up on Benno and the Girl.

The Girl is alone. She is dancing to a very ugly, fifties rock and roll tune. She sings along for a moment. Benno stares out, abstracted.

GIRL: Last night I dreamed I was eating a boiled chicken leg. I started by licking it. I made my tongue all wet and slobbered all over it, up and down, up and down, all around. Then, with my front teeth, I tore off the leg's tip. It was a piece of skin, yellow. I rolled the skin under my teeth, sucking all the juice out of it. Then, I spit it out. Then, suddenly, I stuck all my teeth into the middle of the leg and let it dangle in my mouth. Not biting, not chewing, just letting it dangle.

(*She freezes in place. The light on her dims but does not go out. A tape of the ugly rock tune is heard. On the tape, the Girl is singing very softly into a closely held microphone. The sound is breathy and wet. Then the tape fades very slowly under the following*)

BENNO: (*He starts slowly, with little expression*) Benno loved to draw. And he loved drawings. As soon as he was old enough he stole car fare from his mother's purse and went to the big museum. He snuck in. He ran to the Renaissance paintings. And he stared at them. He stared at their designs, most particularly at their designs. And at their colors. But the designs to begin with were the most significant to him. The circle, for instance, fascinated him; and the right angle as used in a painting like "The Last Supper" thrilled him. He would trace the angles and the circles in these paintings with his fingers when the guards weren't looking. Then, on paper napkins and the dirty lined paper from the Catholic school, he would make designs like those. He drew arcs and circles, and angles and lines trying to vary them with the deception and subtlety of the masters. He wasn't interested in drawing people. He knew what they looked like. Think of the structure of the foot. The lines bend, then they curve. The arch juts up, then juts down; two angles, like a roof. Underneath there is the inverse. The sole is like a barreled vault. Then, at the front, five straight lines—but with rounded tips. Benno drew idealized feet, or distorted them in his own way. He was not interested in the imperfections of real feet. Benno's make be-lieve feet were curved or gracefully inclined. Real feet are crooked and crushed. One day, out of guilt, Benno's Pop-pop bought him a paint set with a Social Security check that bounced or something and caused some discomfort. Benno painted—he colored in his designs. He painted hour upon hour upon hour. He lulled himself asleep planning paintings as though they were battle campaigns. He dreamed colored designs and designs of colors and waking, tried to copy these. Once, once when he had finished painting six straight lines carefully, he stared at his painting and heard . . . heard music played up the back of his spine. It made no difference. When he had finished a painting, Benno was still fat, ugly, and alone. Noth-ing makes a difference, nothing alters anything. It took Benno a very long time to learn this. And Benno wasn't sure he had learned it, re-ally, until he started eating himself to death. Then Benno knew he had learned. For all that matters is the taste of our own flesh. It tastes horrible, particularly if we are fat and sweat a lot. But there are no disappointments there; and those feelings of horror and disgust at chewing ourselves are the only feelings we can be sure of. Benno will put his eyes out soon. Then there will be no seductive angles or circles. Benno will be left to stumble about his filthy room, the windows nailed shut, biting at himself. Thank you.

(*The lights go out on Benno. They intensify on the Girl, who starts singing and dancing again*)

GIRL: So anyway, then I dreamed that I tore off the bite in my mouth. Just then I was woke up by my brother screaming. He sleeps in the bed next to mine. His underpants were covered in jit. He'd had a wet dream.

(*She sniggers*)

He didn't know what it was. I did. I didn't tell him what it was. He started crying. He thought he was gonna die. I let him think so. I'm hungry. I hope mom serves chicken soon.

BLACKOUT

SCENE SIX

The lights come up on Benno and on the Park.

The Girl and Old Man are lying down. The light is heavy and shadowy.

OLD MAN: (*Looks off, nervous*) Damn kids! Make a lotta noise. Benno, why you not play wit them?

BENNO: (*High voice*) What Pop-pop?

OLD MAN: Why you no have friends, Benno? Why you always around me?

BENNO: (*High voice*) I love you, Pop-pop.

(*The Girl laughs, mocking*) I do love you Pop-pop.

OLD MAN: (*To Benno*) Shut up, you crazy you. If you gonna stay around be quiet. Stay over there.

BENNO: (*High voice*) I'm drawing Pop-pop. I'll be quiet.

(*The Old Man draws closer to the Girl and whispers in her ear*)

OLD MAN: You very pretty for an Irish girl. I like you hair, it is so long and thick. And you thighs, they very soft. When I touch them, I feel them long time after.

GIRL: You have bumps on your feet. And there's somethin' strange on your heels. It's like moss.

OLD MAN: You fingers is beautiful. You toes is beautiful.
(*Sucks on her fingers*)

BENNO: (*High voice*) Pop-pop . . .

OLD MAN: (*Very annoyed*) Benno, go 'way! I'm tellin' you, go 'way. Go over to them boys in the trees over there. Go play wit them. You hear me, Benno? Go on!
(*Gets up and mimes chasing Benno away. Benno reacts facially in place. The Old Man, looking off as though following Benno with his eyes*) Maybe they be friends for him.

GIRL: Benno's so fat.

OLD MAN: He's my oldest grandchild.

GIRL: He's a monster. Ooooo! He's so ugly. Benno Blimpie, we call him.

OLD MAN: Lemme get on topa you.

GIRL: No, use your fingers like you did yesterday.

OLD MAN: I wanna do somethin' different.

GIRL: Somethin' different?
(*Caresses his thigh*)
What? I don't wanna do nothin' different.
(*Strikes her tongue in his mouth*)

OLD MAN: I gotta do somethin' different.

GIRL: What?

OLD MAN: Somethin'. You like it.

GIRL: What'll you give me?

OLD MAN: My Social Security check comes next week. I give you if you let me.

GIRL: How much?

OLD MAN: Sixty-two twenty.

GIRL: Bring it next week. We'll see then. Use your fingers today.

OLD MAN: (*Reaches under her dress*) Like this?

GIRL: (*Spreads her legs*) Yes.

OLD MAN: Touch me.

(*The Girl starts to unzip him. Benno screams*)

Damn it to hell! That's Benno.

(*They both look off and the Old Man rises*)

GIRL: It's them boys. They got him.

OLD MAN: Shit!

(*Starts to go off*)

GIRL: (*Holds him back*) Don't go. They're just playin'. That's how boys play nowadays. Come on. Use your fingers today. Next week bring me the check. Kiss me.

OLD MAN: Like this?

(*Kisses her*)

GIRL: Use your fingers.

OLD MAN: (*Reaching under her dress*) Like this?

GIRL: (*Unzipping him*) Yes . . . yes . . .

BENNO: (*Screaming as though terrified and in pain*) Pop-pop! Pop-pop! Pop-pop!

(*Blackout. Benno continues screaming for a beat in the dark. Then silence*)

SCENE SEVEN

Lights up on the kitchen and on Benno.

The Father hovers about the stove.

FATHER: Goddammit, Benno, quit followin' me. Where did she keep things, Benno? You know where that bitch, God forgive me, kept everything? Aw—how would you know? Sit down. How many eggs you want, Benno? Six enough? Benno, I make seven, that should fill us both. I hope she dies in that filthy Napolitan shack livin' with her virgin sister. Get the black pepper, Benno—don't spill it—watch out, don't spill it. Be careful, or you'll spill it; watch out . . . shit fire, you spilled it! Why are you so clumsy, my son?

(*Stoop down as though picking black pepper up off the floor*)

Hey! I know what. I'll put pepperoni in the eggs. That's always good!

(*Sings as he mimes adding the ingredients*)

"Pepperoni hits the spot, helps you shit because it's hot." Why didn't you fight back, Benno, hanh? Why didn't you fight back? I heard, I heard, Benno, what them kids did to you. Why did you lay there like some queer? Hanh! I'll turn the heat up just a tidge. And maybe we better put some milk. Is there somethin' wrong with you my son? Are you a pansy, my son? Why ain't you out there in the street, playin' ball, roughin' up like I did? Why you always in here with you mama, like a girl? Shit, the eggs is stickin' to the pan, I'll stir them. We better put a tidge of sugar in. There. Why are you so fat, my son? Why don't you exercise? I'd never of let them kids near me when I was your age. I'll put some oregano in. Never. I'll tell you, I was a holy terror, a holy terror, geez. I'd have kicked them inna balls, like this. I'd have beat them with my fists, like this. I was no fatty, no pansy. I'd have punched them. I'd have beaten them senseless.

(*Dances around as though in a boxing ring*)

Left, right, left, right and a kick to the balls.

(*Mimes a fight*)

Take that, mother-fucker, take that and that! A right to the side of the head—pow! A left to the jaw and boop! —a knee between the legs! And another left and another right—he's down, he's bleedin'—my God! —he's out! Hey! Hey!

(*Runs to the stove*)

Shit! Shit fire and save the matches! The eggs is burned.

BLACKOUT

SCENE EIGHT

Lights up on Benno and on the Girl. Near her is a small night table with stained and sticky looking bottles and jars on it.

When the lights hits her she sprays a large amount of very smelly hair spray on her hair, then teases her hair violently. Then she smears an enormous amount of purple lipstick on sensuously puffed out lips. During this she sings a very ugly rock tune and occasionally does a dance step to it.

GIRL: Last night I spilled spaghetti all over me. The sauce went over my white blouse and my blue dress; and it was thick sauce with peppers and bits of meat in it. It was a big mess. And Donny, my cousin, wiped it off. He's spiffy. Twenty and in the navy. He took his napkin, it had red stains from his mouth on it and wiped my blouse off. Wiped and wiped, not too hard but strong. Then he took another napkin, my brother's, and wiped my dress off. Wiped and wiped, makin' a small circle in my lap. Donny has big hands, a lotta hair on them around the knuckles and the veins is very thick. His fingers is thick, too, and the middle one is long and heavy. I dream about Donny's hand makin' circles in my lap.
(Freezes in place. The light on her dims)
BENNO: Benno grew up thinking that talent and sensitivity were things people took seriously. At least, that important people took seriously—artists, for instance, and teachers. Benno grew up hoping that looks and sex didn't matter. That paintings would satisfy any longing he'd ever have. And when that longing got too strong, a quick pulling with the palm would be enough. Benno was wrong. Benno has been heard to say that nothing matters save the taste of his own flesh. But since then, time has passed. For your benefit he has conjured up scenes better not remembered. And Benno realizes that he was guilty of over-simplification. There are things that mat-

ter: looks matter, sex matters. These are all that matter. Benno feels that those who deny this are participating in a huge joke. Benno has learned his lesson. Paintings, you see, aren't enough. When loneliness and emptiness and longing congeal like a jelly nothing assuages the ache. Nothing, nothing, nothing. It was the end of spring, the traditional season of youth, renewal and young love. Benno returned to his old neighborhood, having celebrated his twentieth birthday. He found the poorest side street in his old neighborhood. Fitzgerald Street, by name. And he rented a room on the third floor of a row house on Fitzgerald Street. Benno nailed shut all the windows in that room, even though it was summer. Something about imbibing his own smell. Benno is not as isolated as you might think. He hears the horrible street noises. He hears the monster children screaming. He even allows himself to have his shade up one-half hour a day. Today at one p.m., Benno had his shade up. He stared out his nailed window, stared through the caked dirt that streaks the window's glass. He saw a wild circle flashing red across the street. He stared at that circle and was tempted to . . . never mind. He was tempted and stared and was tempted some more. And then he saw the agent of that circle. It was a little girl. A beautiful little girl. Oh yes, Benno knows beauty. He knows if he tells you. Once, when he saw something beautiful, it would flash across his eyes like a hot knife and he would peer, eyes stuck there until they ached. Once, he tells you, no longer. For beauty has lost his power over me, it has lost its power, no more beauty, no more longing to grasp it within me and smother it with my bulk, please God, no more beauty.

(*He is almost weeping. He eats passionately and slowly pulls himself together*)

GIRL: (*Unfreezes and continues with her makeup*) When Donny finished wiping me off, I smiled up at him and his eyes, they're black, got very big. When ma wasn't looking, I let my fingers take a walk along his thigh. I saw the big bump in the middle of his thigh get bigger. Then, when ma was clearin' the table, I spilled the plate of meatballs all over me. While she was in the kitchen, Donny licked them off with his tongue. Ma caught him and gave him hell.

Pop laughed. Donny ran into the bathroom and puked all over, like a sissy. I changed my mind about Donny. I think Donny is a jerk-off. (*Lights out on Girl*)

BENNO: Benno has decided: He will no longer lift the shade, he will no longer look out into the street. Benno stayed in this tiny room. He left every two days to buy food. Otherwise he never went out. Except in cases of emergency such as when the ice cream truck came along. He did nothing. He ate continually from when he awoke until he fell asleep. He did nothing save remember. When I become so fat I cannot get into his clothes and can barely move, I will nail the door shut. I will put his eyes out with a long nail and I will bite at himself until he dies. In the middle of this filthy hole on the third floor of a row house in the poorest side street of my old neighborhood there will I be: A mountain of flesh. There are rats in this room. I see them slithering along the sides of the wall. They will eat me. These rats will find Benno beautiful. They will long for him. He will be a sexual object to them. They will make the devouring of Benno's body an erotic act. They will gnaw hollows into his face, into his belly. And in those hollows, they will fornicate. Then, they will perish. The instant before he is ready to die, Benno will swallow a huge draught of poison. These rats in eating Benno will be eating poisoned meat. The poison will cause a fearful splitting of stomachs, vital rat organs will swell up and burst even while the rats are making love. Even while they are eating. Posthumously, Benno will have been loved.

BLACKOUT

SCENE NINE

Lights up on Park and on Benno.

The Girl and the Old Man are seated together on the ground. The Old Man has a wine bottle in a paper bag with him and takes swigs from it. The Girl is in a Catholic schoolgirl's uniform—white blouse, blue, rather long skirt and white ankle socks with blue oxfords. She has a school satchel nearby.

OLD MAN: Benno, you stay over there and draw. Don' bother me. You old enough to go pee-wee by yourself.

GIRL: He's funny, retarded.

OLD MAN: You hear me, Benno?

BENNO: (*High voice*) Yes, Pop-pop.

GIRL: (*Mimicking*) Yes, Pop-pop.

OLD MAN: Just be sure you stay away! An' don' you go tellin' you bitch mother, either.

BENNO: (*High voice*) I won't, Pop-pop.

GIRL: Queerie!

OLD MAN: You hear me good, Benno. Leave me alone today.

BENNO: (*High voice*) Yes, Pop-pop. (*Quietly to himself, high voice*)
I love you, Pop-pop.
(*Normal voice, to the audience*) And Benno wept. He didn't realize at that time that there is nothing funnier than a fat boy, weeping. Nothing funnier. Nothing.
(*A pause. He laughs dryly. The light dims somewhat on Benno. But he stares at the scene intently*)

OLD MAN: (*Takes a drink, offers the bottle to the Girl*) Drink this!

GIRL: Don' wan' none.

OLD MAN: Drink.

GIRL: Don' wan' none, I said!
(*Takes a long swig and grimaces*)
Ooooooooh! What is it?

OLD MAN: La vita, carina, la vita.

GIRL: Don' know Eyetalian. You bring the check?

OLD MAN: Sixty-two twenty.

GIRL: Lemme see.

OLD MAN: Later.

GIRL: Lemme see.

(*He reaches into his back pocket, and presents her with the check. She scrutinizes it*) Yeah . . . yeah . . . sixty-two twenty. Sign it over to me.

OLD MAN: What do you mean?

GIRL: You know what I mean. Sign it over.

OLD MAN: Can't write.

GIRL: Make yer sign.

OLD MAN: Got no pencil.

GIRL: Got one in my school bag.

(*Reaches into her school bag and removes a pencil*)

New point. Come on.

OLD MAN: All right.

(*Makes his mark on the check. The Girl reaches for the wine and takes a long pull*)

GIRL: (*As he notices her drinking*) Didn't have no lunch today. On a diet. Give it to me.

OLD MAN: Afta.

(*Puts check in his back pocket*)

GIRL: Benno hangs around you a lot. Why? He ain't normal.

OLD MAN: Kiss me.

GIRL: My brother beat him up, broke his glasses. Said he wanted to crush his nose against his face like a pimple.

OLD MAN: Touch me.

GIRL: You love Benno?

OLD MAN: Let me do it now, I be gentle.

GIRL: Do you love him?

OLD MAN: I take you top off.

GIRL: (*Twists away*) Yesterday my brother told me he gonna beat Benno up afta school on Monday. You gonna try and stop him?

OLD MAN: Help me wit you buttons.

GIRL: Not yet. Use your fingers.

OLD MAN: Want more today. Help me with the buttons.

GIRL: (*He tries to start undressing the Girl. She resists but in a lazy teasing way. The Old Man sometimes stops trying to remove her top and caresses her*) Why is Benno so weird? Drawing all the time. Never playin' in the street? In school on Tuesday—c'mon, cut it out—he started talkin' about this Eyetalian painter. Just started talking; sister didn't call on him or nothing. Cut that out. Then Benno showed us his drawings. They was weird. One was supposed to be a old man. He was long and thin with these blurry features. Looked like my brother's dickie floatin' in the bathtub. Stop it! I don't like you slobbering on me!

OLD MAN: Drink some more.
(*Takes a long swig and passes her the bottle*)

GIRL: Lick my feet like you did before.
(*Drinks*)

OLD MAN: I want more—I want more.
(*Gets on top of her*)

BENNO: (*High voice, loudly*) Pop-pop, look what I drew. Look, see the circles . . .

OLD MAN: (*Jumping off the Girl*) God damn it to hell, Benno! Get away from here, go on!
(*Acts as though chasing Benno off*)
Damn kid, always around, always in the way. (*Lies down beside the Girl*)

GIRL: (*Giggles*) Benno couldn't genuflect at mass on Wednesday. He couldn't get that far down. And when he did get down on his knees, he couldn't get up. Even sister laughed. Then we all had to go to confession for laughing at mass. Even sister. I smelled the priest in the confessional. All sweaty and underarmy. But nice. Do you love Benno?

OLD MAN: (*Caressing her, kissing her hair*) You carina, you I love; all of you. Fine Irish hair and the little hairs down there. I wanna scoop you up with my mouth. You hear me, with my mouth!

I wanna bury my teeth, bury them, in there, in and in and in. Come to me, cara, I ready. I wan' . . .

GIRL: (*Squirming away*) You wanna, you wanna, you wanna! You're drunk, you're a slob!

OLD MAN: I wan' more from you this time, this time more!

GIRL: Hey, hey!

(*He reaches under her dress*)

I'm not in the mood!

(*She reaches for the bottle and takes a long swig*)

OLD MAN: (*Lies back and strokes her*) In the paese, over there, over the seas, I took a little girl inna wood. I was how old? Nineteen maybe, who knows? I take her inna the wood and swallow her whole. You hear, swallow her whole?! I start at her feet.

(*Grabs the Girl's foot. She utters an annoyed cry*)

Took her toes inna my mouth and bite them off, one by one. Then I bite inna her leg.

(*Grabs her leg and holds it tight while she struggles*) and chew onna the bone. It was hard that bone, but then, then I have good teeth and chew hard. I ate all of her, and today, today I wan' more . . .

(*The Girl finally pushes him away with all her strength*)

GIRL: No! I'm sick of you and your yellow skin and your sores and your smell!

OLD MAN: (*Trying to get on top of her*) Bella mia, mia bella, ti voglio! I wanna dig inna you skin!

GIRL: (*Twisting away*) Dago shit! Smelly!

BENNO: (*High voice*) Pop-pop! Pop-pop!

(*The Old Man has begun to chase the Girl, reaching out for her. This has started slowly but becomes wild. The old Man starts gasping for breath and getting dizzy. High voice*) Why are you running like that, Pop-pop? Stop it, I'm scared!

GIRL: (*Dodging the Old Man as though it were a game*) Grandson's a queerie, granddad's a smelly!

OLD MAN: (*Still chasing her, panting*) I wan' more, more!

BENNO: (*High voice*) Please, Pop-pop!

GIRL: Smelly!

BENNO: (*High voice*) Leave her alone, Pop-pop!

OLD MAN: (*Gasping*) Mia! Bella mia, ti voglio! Fermati! T'amo!

GIRL: Wop bastard!

(*The Old Man lunges and catches the Girl. She utters a cry and fights him. Neither is playful. The Old Man throws her to the ground. She screams. He tries to hurl himself on top of her but she moves at the last minute and he hits the ground with a thud and a cry. He is stunned briefly*)

BENNO: (*High voice*) Oh! Oh, Pop-pop . . .

(*The Girl runs to the wine bottle and breaks it*)

GIRL: (*Waving the broken bottle*) Come on, dago shit, come on!

OLD MAN: (*Laughs*) Tigra, tigra, come on, tigra!

(*They circle each other slowly. Occasionally the Girl strikes out at the Old Man. He is playful but she is very serious. From his stool Benno watches in terror*)

BENNO: Pop-pop, should I run for the police?

OLD MAN: (*To the Girl, still circling*) I wanna chew you up!

GIRL: Asshole!

(*Lunges again and cuts him on the arm*)

OLD MAN: (*Yells but chases her more violently*) Mia, vieni!

BENNO: Leave her alone, Pop-pop, she's crazy!

(*The Old Man acts as though Benno is tugging at him and turns to push him away*)

OLD MAN: Go home, queerie, go home! Today I wan' more . . .

(*With a scream the Girl lunges and stabs the Old Man in the back with the broken bottle. He screams and falls. Screaming*) Aiuto, aiuto, Benno, help me! (*He twists desperately in the mud as though trying to stop the pain in his back. Benno gasps, then stares. The Girl also stares wide-eyed. The Old Man continues to scream and throws up in the mud*)

GIRL: (*In a stunned whisper*) Go 'head, puke, you wop bastard!

OLD MAN: (*Almost voiceless*) I . . . I . . . I . . .

(*Dies. There is a pause. The Girl becomes suddenly hysterical*)

GIRL: Bastard! Bastard! Filthy wop bastard! Oh my god, my god, I've . . . I've . . . he's . . .

(*With a cry she throws the bottle down. It shatters. She looks at it frightened, then bends over the corpse, screaming*)

Dago, dago, wop, filthy, dago bastard, bastard, bitch, dago, jerk-off, bitch, mother-fucker, filthy . . . mother . . .

(*She is gasping. She pulls herself together suddenly and looks around*) Geez . . . the check!

(*She searches the body for the check and finds it. She removes it from the back pocket*) Muddy.

(*Wipes the check on her skirt*) Hey . . . hey . . . you kiddin'?

(*Kicks the body*)

Oh . . . oh, Caarist! Hey Benno, your pop-pop's dead. Don't you tell nobody or my brother'll get you good. Oh . . .

(*Looks at the body*) Oh . . . Caarist!

(*Runs off*)

BENNO: (*A pause. Then he whispers, normal voice*) Pop-pop.

BLACKOUT

SCENE TEN

Lights up on Benno and the kitchen. The Father is pacing tensely.

FATHER: Where the hell is your mother, Benno? Hanh? Mary! Mary! Where the hell are you! We should be there! Mary!

MOTHER: (*Offstage*) All right, for Christ's sake, I'm comin'!

FATHER: Jesus Christ—let me make sure everythin' is ready, Benno.

(*Opens ice box*)

Yep, got the spare ribs for the gravy—Uncle Fonse likes them—Benno—don't eat the cake, it's for the relatives, afta.

(*Calling*)

Mary, for Christ's sake, hurry.

MOTHER: (*Off*) Jesus Christ in Heaven shove that friggin' racin' form in that big mouth. I'm comin'!

(*A pause. She enters. She seems ashamed. The dress she is wearing is too small for her. He looks at her*)

FATHER: Jesus—is that all you had to wear?

MOTHER: Ain't had no money to buy a dress in years—

FATHER: Well, at least they'll know you was Benno's mother and you eat well—wear a shawl or somethin'. Come on.

MOTHER: Not yet.

FATHER: Oh, Jesus!

MOTHER: I ain't ready yet! Gotta get inna the mood. I don't like wakes. You go, I'll come later. Not ready I tell you.

FATHER: And the kid?

MOTHER: Why can't you take him, you ashamed? You think they'll think he's my fault if he comes in wit me? Hanh? Is that what you think? Oh, their little Dominick could never commit somethin' like this flabby monster. He could never cause such ugliness to come inna the world. It's Mary's fault.

FATHER: Look you, none of your shit tonight. You keep that big ugly Napolitan mouth shut. And you bring the kid. It's my father's wake and I want you to show some respect, or so help me God, I'll take the strap to you right there.

MOTHER: All right, all right, get the hell out.

FATHER: Make sure that kid keeps decent too. (*Exits*)

MOTHER: Let's have some coffee, Benno. I need it.

(*Heats coffee*) Oh Jesus, Jesus, how'm I gonna face it? All them relatives of his: his sister Edith, that witch of a prune face, faccia brutt', Virgine, ti conosci', Benno stop slobberin', and his brother, Basil—face like a rhinoceros' ass—how'm I gonna face them? They hate me. They look down on me—Mary the peasant, they call me. But it was me, the virgin knows, me, Mary the horse, put the old

man up. Me! I hadda see him come and spit inna the sink every day.
Me! And I hadda run the vacuum cleaner to get the scales from his
sores. Those damn scales were everywhere, like fairy dust. I even
found 'em on the window sill. How did they get on the window sill?
What did he do, scratch them while watchin' some broad walk
down the street? And do they thank me for cleanin' up afta him
week afta friggin' week? Nah! Benno, why you puttin' five tea-
spoons of sugar in you coffee, hanh? Why can't you put two like a
human being? Three, even three I could see, God knows, but five?
Who do you take afta? Hanh?

(*Gets up and pours coffee for herself*)

Take some coffee, Mary. Weep into them grounds. And them God
damned lousy shits look down at me. My father, my friggin' father,
God rest his soul, was eight times, nah, nine times the man theirs
was! Nine times, you hear me? The day before he died I went a see
him. Couldn't find him. Where was he, where? Then, suddenly, I
hear this clang, this loud clang. CLANG! It come from the cellar. I
run down. There he is, seventy-six, at least, chasin' rats with the
shovel. He screamed: Ecco! Ecco! And then he smashes one with the
shovel. CLANG!! It splattered all over the cellar. That was a real
man. Not a ball-less bum like you no good bastard father. Well, have
a cookie Mary, you deserve it.

(*To Benno*)

No more for you, dinosaur, you've had seven. No more, I said. You
shit, you!

(*Pantomimes reaching over and slapping his hand. Benno winces in
place, as though fighting back tears*)

Cry baby! Looka him hold back the tears. No good sissy! Men don't
cry. And looka! Just a big lump of lard. Jesus, I could store you up
and cook with you. What did I do, oh virgin, to deserve all this
suffering? Hanh? Looka them pimples. Don't scratch them you no
good! If only you wasn't so flabby. If only you had some muscle on
them monster arms and legs. But all you is, is a huge, flabby rat. You
hear me? A rat; with them big, black dartin' eyes. I'm sick a you;
and sick a that creep you no good bastard father. Who goes out and

works like a dog? Me! Who comes home and cleans like a horse? Hanh? I do! And who put that no good bum, your Pop-pop, God rest his soul, up for years and years and then he has to go out and let some nigger stab him with his own wine bottle and we don't even get his last check, God damn it all to hell, *I* did and *I* do, that's who! Mary! Mary the horse! Mary the horse, they call me—don't take another cookie, you pig—Mary the horse.

(*She is becoming hysterical*)

They used a call me Bella, beautiful, you know that? Beautiful and I had red hair, flaming, and big boobs, almost as big as yours, you little queer, and a shape, Madone', what a shape! Old Joey Fercanti, I coulda married him, said my lips should be on the silver screen, that's how big they were and thick and red. Bella, Bella they called me. And when I danced they look at me and when I walked home from the market even with a dozen other girls, they looked at me and when I got married all the guys in the neighborhood got drunk. Bella! And look at me now—I'm almost as ugly as you, I'm a hag, a bitch! Got no shape no more and my hair's grey and fallin' out and your father, your father that no good lousy son of a bitch did this to me, worked at me and worked at me, a rat, chewin' at me, with big dartin' eyes and tearin' me to pieces! Look at me, look at me good. Oh my God, my God, how did I wind up like this, with the peelin' wallpaper and nothin' else, no furniture, no money, not a decent dress. What am I gonna wear to that wake? They'll laugh, you hear me, they'll laugh.

(*She has reached a frenzy. And sobs for a moment and then slowly begins to calm down. Occasionally her chest heaves from sob. Benno stares wide-eyed. She has calmed down. Slowly she rises and pours herself another cup of coffee*) Have some more coffee, Mary. That's all you got, caffeine, that's all you got in the whole world. (*To Benno.*) And you, monster, you with them big eyes, them big black eyes, what do you want now?

BENNO: (*High, soft voice*) A cookie.

(*Mother sobs. Lights dim on Mother*)

SCENE ELEVEN

Benno speaks urgently to the audience.

BENNO: And what about love? Specifically, what about sexual love? Did or did not this fat one ever have congress with anything other than his palm? Benno wonders: should he describe his sexual past? Benno is ravenous for himself and time it presses on. Benno must cease this night or face yet one other two-day cycle.

(Out of the shadows comes the Old Man. He is dressed in a long butcher's apron. It is abnormally white and quite long. The Old Man's hair has been whitened and so has his face. There is a golden aura about him so that even though he is recognizably a butcher, there is something angelic in his appearance as well. He carries a golden meat cleaver and a black crayon. During the following, as Benno speaks, the Old Man pulls over his head an enormous white robe. When the robe is fully on Benno, the Old Man prepares to draw on it with his crayon. He will draw on Benno a butcher's chart identifying the various slices of meat. Benno submits to all this without paying any attention. Benno speaks laconically and with a certain irony. The light on him becomes brighter and brighter as he speaks) Benno and sex: a story. Benno went out one night. He was fourteen. His pop-pop had been dead—how many years? They blur too much for Benno to know for sure. Had Benno been an intellectual he would have concerned himself with the nature of time. Benno felt that the secret of time was perhaps his secret. Maybe Benno was the product of a time warp. Benno then would have been the bloated issue of an inverted time womb which, due to God joke, or cosmic spasm, vomited him out long before, or long after his true time. But when, he asks you, when would have been Benno's time? Some of us, it seems, exist outside of nature and no one knows where we fit. Nature has her claws in all of you but not in we who exist outside her. You have your claws in us. I see that you all think

Benno speaks nonsense. My mouth is dry. Perhaps what he says to you, even to the very words is unfamiliar. Perhaps it is Hungarian he speaks or some curious combination of frothy diphthongs. Benno always had a problem with his saliva.

(*Out of the dark come the voices of the Father and Mother*)

MOTHER'S VOICE: Not only a fatty, but he drools, too. Looka that: it's like a broken water fountain!

FATHER'S VOICE: Is there something wrong with you, my son?

BENNO: Benno ran out one night. In the best tradition of arts and letters there beat in him the age-old desperation. Benno felt those horrible waves of longing wash over him and tumble back on himself and he could do nothing about it. There was no cure for that longing in Benno. No church socials sponsored his dreams of satiety; no youth organization provided him with a concourse to fulfillment; and double dating was out. There was no cure out of popular sentiment nor out of clinical misassessment. Benno was singular and had to suffer alone. Sometimes I want to run to my nailed windows and vomit out them. The force, the force of my vomit would explode through the window onto the passersby and crush them. And crush them.

(*He pauses for a moment. The Old Man is now ready to draw on him*)

Benno Blimpie: The sensuous fatso. Prefatory to his supper of self.

OLD MAN: Breast! (*Draws the lines around Benno's breast, as a butcher's chart would show them, and labels them*)

BENNO: The fourteen-year-old Benno ran out one night . . .

OLD MAN: Rib!

(*As before, draws the lines and labels them*)

BENNO: Benno was looking for love.

OLD MAN: Chuck!

(*As before, draws and labels lines*)

BENNO: Benno was looking for love!

MOTHER'S VOICE: (*Off. In the dark*) You think we should put him away?

FATHER'S VOICE: Who?

MOTHER'S VOICE: Who else? Our humpback of Notre Dame son!

BENNO: For love.

OLD MAN: Round.

(*As before draws on Benno and labels him*)

BENNO: Benno took a walk. He ended up in Edgar Allan Poe school yard. A place of concrete, broken glass and dog shit. Dried dog shit of the peculiarly urban sort. In the school yard, Benno saw three boys. They lounged about in the shadows, some distance from him. They were older than Benno, from his neighborhood. He saw the school yard to be a place of waste; to be a locus of the city's fecal matter. Yes, he saw that broken glass, that concrete with the brown grass jutting and that hard dog shit to be part of a gigantic fecal mass; yes, and he saw those boys with their tee shirts and torn dungarees also as so many turds. Nor was Benno himself exempt; he too was waste. All was waste. Through the haze of this decay, Benno saw these boys, and chose to wait.

OLD MAN: Sirloin . . .

(*As before, draws, then labels*)

BENNO: In due course, the boys noticed Benno. They performed the usual ritual of greeting Benno. They pointed and giggled.

OLD MAN: Rump.

(*As before, draws, then labels*)

BENNO: Hey kid, one said, hey kid. They beckoned me closer. I went. What you name, kid, they asked. They knew already. Benno, he replied. Hey, they sang out, Benno Blimpie. Hey fellas, meet Benno Blimpie.

OLD MAN: Loin.

(*Draws and labels as before*)

BENNO: The tallest said: Hey Benno, know what this is? He grabbed his crotch. My mouth was dry. Yes, Benno was heard to whisper, I know. They laughed. Hey fellas, they sang out, Benno Blimpie knows.

OLD MAN: Liver.

(*Draws and labels Benno*)

BENNO: The oldest lowered his voice and said: Hey Benno, you wanna eat me?

OLD MAN: Kidney.

(*Draws and labels Benno*)

BENNO: I said nothing. Sure he does, one said. Benno wants to eat us all. The oldest said: Sure, Benno wants a big meal, he wants to eat us all. They settled the order, one taking watch, one watching me, the other being served. They pushed me down, it took all three. And one after the other I ate them. I ate all three.

OLD MAN: Heart.

(*Labels and draws on Benno*)

BENNO: I ate all three. One, two and three. I caught on after a bit. They were happy during it and pranced around. They enjoyed it. When Benno had finished all three, they bloodied his nose and forced one eye shut by pounding it. Then they picked up pieces of glass and dried dog shit and stuffed them into Benno's bleeding mouth. Laughing, they ran off. I was left lying like a blimp in the middle of the public school yard. In the middle of all that concrete, with come and shit and glass in my mouth. I couldn't cry; Benno couldn't scream. He lay there; and in that instant, time stopped. And feeling, it stopped too, and seemed to merge with time, and with space. My sense of identity seeped out of me into the cracks in the concrete. And for a few seconds I was out of myself, totally free of myself. Totally. Free. Free. And this I call: The Transfiguration of Benno Blimpie.

SCENE TWELVE

Lights come up intensely on everyone. The Old Man hands Benno the meat cleaver.

OLD MAN: You ready now!

(*Slowly, Benno rises from his chair with great effort. He raises the meat cleaver. Everyone turns and watches him in silence*)

BENNO: I am Benno. I am eating myself to death.

(*Slowly he lowers the meat cleaver as though to cut off some part of himself. The others watch intently. As he reaches that part, quick blackout*)

AFTERWORD

Explication of his play by a playwright should be unnecessary; if his writing is any good, the work ought to be clear enough from a performance or a reading. For better or worse *Benno Blimpie* and *Gemini* appear to me lucid.

Nonetheless, here I would like to answer in print some of those questions which are often asked me about the plays and state what at the moment are my particular interests aesthetically with an end to clarifying, not the plays themselves, but perhaps where they stand stylistically in that confusing swamp called the "modern theatre."

One of the more frequently occurring questions is how I came to start these plays.

Most of my plays begin with strong visual images that can be mined theatrically, so to speak. They are often detailed and imply important occurrences that can lead to theatrical complications or demand dramatic development.

As it happens, I dreamed *Benno Blimpie*—or at least dreamed memorably and in detail the visual aspects of the play. I saw in the dream a stage; on it, dead center, an enormous, fat boy. To his right was a city park, one of those mysterious and rather sinister effusions of greenery cramped between concrete. In the park was an old man, clearly related to the boy. To the boy's left was a kitchen such as might be found in a row house, and in the kitchen, his parents. I also saw, in less clear relationship, a teen-aged girl in a dirty Catholic school uniform. She was playing in the park. I knew that in some way the fat boy was the subject of the conversations and certain actions of the others, that they loathed him, and that he was keenly aware of their loathing.

I still remember this dream—the strong visual image was very rich in implications. Although the fat boy was perhaps eighteen or twenty, he was also simultaneously a child, playing near his grandfather in the park and overhearing the grandfather's lascivious courtship of the young girl. It was as though I were sharing in the fat boy's mystical ability to exist on different planes at once, to be simultaneously active in the present and the past. And I knew that for him there would be no future.

About six years later, while working as a messenger in New York, I had a fantasy. I saw two very beautiful young people—a boy and girl—climbing over a backyard fence such as I had often seen in South Philadelphia to surprise a mutual friend from college with whom both were involved. I saw the alley, the two adjoining yards, and sensed the aura, so to speak, of the neighbors and the neighborhood, and in a flash knew the story and style of the piece. This, of course, was *Gemini*.

There are those who question the ending of *Gemini*, wondering whether it has for example ideological or didactic implications beyond being a theatrically effective ending for a comedy.

The answer is no. I do not see this ending as a "cop out," nor do I see it affirming heterosexuality as a life-style chosen by the hero at the ninth hour, nor do I see the reverse as true, nor is the ending meant to be ironic, or to parody affirmative endings. I think the meaning of the ending is transparent: a young man who is in the main heterosexual (Francis has had girl friends before Judith) but who has had some self-doubts (as anyone might who is bookish and intellectual but from a working-class neighborhood and is perhaps insecure about his appearance) elects to continue a more or less successful relationship with a girl to whom he is well suited, and who is well suited to him. The ending is happy because Francis chooses to work with a realistic situation, despite possible problems, rather than chasing off after a potentially destructive fantasy.

As to endings in general: many writers on the theatre like to debate them, but in fact a successful ending is not one that can be simply tacked on to make a play commercial. After all, a writer may wish to end his play happily but be unable to. It would certainly have been out of the question to end *Benno* with that character going on the water diet and losing twenty pounds his first week; even if some very fat people, after lives like Benno's, have found salvation in radical fad diets. Just so a sad ending can appear forced or affected. Should Francis commit suicide at the end of *Gemini*—a solution that appears to satisfy the fantasies or desires of certain lugubrious individuals? Of course not, for from the first scene it is the given of the play that his problem is neither unthinkable nor insoluble.

A further question that sometimes arises concerns what style the plays are meant to be in, and where their author stands in the confusing welter of poses, manners, ideologies that confuse the issue so totally in contemporary theatre criticism.

The style of these plays clearly misses elements of "realism" with the operatic, even the surreal. Yet, in the long run, despite "arias," and sections where naturalistic narrative propulsion is held up for the expansion of an almost musical moment, my hope has been that the characters and situations would be above all believable and engage the sympathy and recognition of the audience.

I certainly went through my period of writing esoteric plays that danced above the concerns and understanding of most people. But I have deliberately changed my way of thinking about the theatre.

I have come to feel that above all the theatre is a popular art form, that theatre is meant to be among the most accessible and readily understandable of the arts; and in fact must be, if there is to be a functioning, meaningful theatre. When there was no popular theatre, what have come to be known as "closet dramas" were written to be read by devotees in a literary circle. But where theatre has flourished it has done so for a large and multivarious audience. It is for this reason that there is low comedy as well as high tragedy in Shakespeare, that Ibsen left the trolls in the hills for those in the drawing room, following *Peer Gynt* with *Ghosts* and *Hedda Gabler*.

It seems to me the goal of most great theatre artists has been to be understood. This is not to say that there are no great plays which require thought and acquaintance, nor to suggest that intellect and reason have no place in the theatre. However, the central discipline and greatest challenge to the theatre writer has always been, in my estimation, to make clear, strong, and accessible that which he has chosen as a theme. The more complex, the more difficult the theme, the greater the challenge, and when it works, the greater the art. It is not only the grand concept, the structural audacity of *King Lear* we admire, but the extraordinary artistry with which the difficult, the complex, the mysterious is made immediate and moving, the unequivocal way the most elusive speculations about existence are theatricalized, demonstrated, without however being produced or sentimentalized.

Of course, *Benno* and *Gemini* are not doctrinaire plays written to make a critical point. But, they can stand as my declarations against an increasing trend among American critics to enshrine the needlessly confusing. These critics often assume it is hard to mystify an audience; actually there is nothing easier; clarity, what I would call meaningful accessibility (quite the opposite of pablum), is always the hardest to accomplish.